Sojourns of the Soul:

A Guide to Transformation

A journey guided by
JONAH and RAPHAEL

by Kim D. Koenig

Assistance by Robin O'Brien

Uni ★ Sun
Kansas City

Copyright ©1989 by Kim D. Koenig

All rights reserved. No part of this work may be reproduced or transmitted in any form or by any means, electronic or mechanical, including photocopying and recording, or by any information storage and retrieval system, except as may be expressly permitted by the 1976 Copyright Act or in writing by the publisher.

Cover art "Emerging" by Mark J. Adams.
Book design by Pat Huyett
Request for such permission should be addressed to:

Uni ★ Sun
P.O. Box 25421
Kansas City, MO 64119

This book is manufactured in the United States of America. Distribution by The Talman Company:

The Talman Co.
150 Fifth Avenue
New York, NY 10011

Library of Congress Cataloging-in-Publication Data

Koenig, Kim, 1956–
    Sojourns of the soul: a guide to transformation by Kim Koening.
        p.   cm.
    ISBN 0-912949-26-0: $8.95
    1. Spirit writing.   I. Title.
BF1301.K64   1989
133.9'3—dc20   89-51921
                                                                                    CIP

Dear Marc,

Hint: the first one is on page three.

*   *   *

*With Love, to the part of You
that is Me, from the part of
Me that is You.*

*   *   *

Warm thoughts,

Love,
Koenig

5/91

Contents

Contents

Foreword

A year before I dictated this book I was a devoted criminal defense lawyer. I was actively involved in the defense of murder, robbery and rape cases. Becoming a trial lawyer had been the fulfillment of a lifelong dream. I was a public defender and I felt tremendous passion for defending the downtrodden of our society. I was wholeheartedly committed to fighting for justice for the powerless. The work was very exciting. Criminal trials involve the kinds of things that television shows are made of: Mystery. Intrigue. Conflict. Tension. Violence.

The work was also very stressful. The freedom of human beings was in my hands. My body was in constant physical pain. I had daily headaches. My muscles felt like rocks. I was constantly fatigued, despite the fact I ate decent food, exercised, and meditated regularly. I lived in a peaceful house on an island with a loving husband. I had the best of friends, took exotic vacations and enjoyed life to the fullest in every conceivable way. Or so I thought.

After six years of trial work, I started listening to myself talk. Over and over again, I heard myself sigh heavily when people asked me how I was doing. I would respond that "I" was fine, but I didn't *feel* good. I began to notice that I never *felt* good, yet intellectually speaking I was doing fine. My work was very gratifying to the ego. It involved me emotionally. My personal life was deeply satisfying. So what was missing? Why was my body ill? Was my soul speaking to me through my body?

In August 1985 I walked out of the courthouse following the verdict in a four-count aggravated murder case. I knew my life was going to change. I could no longer ignore the fact that something I had worked for all my life, and loved passionately, didn't make me feel good.

My client in the case was a likeable man. Yet he was convicted of murdering the woman he loved. In the process another woman was killed, and two others were seriously wounded, one paralyzed and confined to a wheelchair for life. The trial, which lasted for many weeks, followed months and months of preparation. The defense was insanity. Such a defense forces one to examine deep aspects of human consciousness. Other passionate issues were also involved—religious repression, racism and the Vietnam War.

I derived some sense of satisfaction from the case in recognizing that the State had not persisted in an attempt to kill my client through the imposition of the death penalty. Yet the conclusion of the trial left two people dead, one confined to a wheelchair, another wounded, and a client I had grown to care for, sentenced to life in prison without the possibility of parole. I recognized that the system I worked within had few winners.

September came. It was fall. Change was in the air. There was something about the air that I wanted to understand. I wanted to breathe deeply, to fill myself up with air. Perhaps I was in search of the feeling of spirit. I began a "light" meditation class in Seattle. The class was taught by a man named John Jennings. I surrounded myself with people who thought in a metaphysical manner. Yes, metaphysical—beyond the physical.

I had always known there was something beyond the physical. I was eminently aware of that, yet having responsibility for the lives of 80 people in any given day, left me without a lot of time to ponder such ethereal matters.

I remembered back to my childhood days and the slumber parties we had had as kids. I remembered being ten years old and being lifted off the ground by several children as they put only their fingers under my body. I remembered the rustle of the leaves of the tree in my face. It felt perfectly natural to be "floating" off the ground. This was the first conscious memory I had that led me to believe physical matter was not all it appeared to be.

I remembered being 18 years old and playing with the Ouija board with college friends. At first I thought it was rather strange, but soon relished the moments when I could speak with the "consciousness" of a friend or relative many miles away.

I remembered being 19 years old and meeting a man named Earl Robinson. When I met Earl he was in his late sixties. He had a fit body, gray hair, sparkling eyes, and a beard. He is one of the most lively and spirited people I have ever known. Earl is also a very gifted songwriter. His passionate beliefs are often expressed in his songs. He wrote the famous folksong "Joe Hill" as a salute to the labor organizer killed by the State following an alleged murder frame-up during the thirties. The song was recorded by Joan Baez. To celebrate the Supreme Court decision on school desegregation in the fifties he wrote the song "Black and White" which was recorded by Three Dog Night.

Earl and I were brought together through our common feelings of love for one great man—Supreme Court Justice William O. Douglas. As a law student, Justice

Douglas' opinions often brought tears to my eyes and a chill to my spine. I was especially moved by his dissent in the *Sierra Club v. Morton* case. In his opinion he urged that trees, rivers and animal life should have constitutional rights. Earl's admiration for Justice Douglas inspired him to write a musical for the man called *Ride the Wind*. I met Earl at a seminar in honor of Justice Douglas where he was performing this piece of music.

Earls life reads like a fascinating book. Among other things he was blacklisted by Hollywood in the fifties. He had dinner and performed at the White House several times during the Roosevelt administration. He has a close affinity to and communicates with dolphins. It was through Earl Robinson that I became acquainted with the process of channeling.

Channeling involves allowing oneself to open up one's energy centers to let the transmittal and reception of information come from other planes of reality. A spiritual being makes him/herself present in the form of energy, and uses the "channel's" vocal chords to deliver information and knowledge to those there to receive it.

In 1977, Earl invited me to a live channeling session at his home in Santa Barbara. There I met William Rainen, who channeled a being named Dr. Peebles. My first impression of channeling was that it was rather bizarre, but very interesting. Mr. Rainen closed his eyes and went into a meditation. Soon another persona permeated his being. His body seemed to expand. His voice changed octaves. The pace and intonation of his speech was different. The electrifying energy of Dr. Peebles filled the air. The intensity of the vibration was overwhelming. I could not deny that I was in the presence of an energy I had never felt before. What I remember most about Dr.

Peebles was his directness, his humor, his love and the uplifting quality of the counsel he imparted.

Earl then hired me to transcribe some channeled tapes for him, so I was exposed to even more channeled material. Thus began my "intellectual" introduction to channeling.

This intellectual understanding of channeling turned into an experiential understanding in the spring of 1980. I was a second- year law student at the University of Puget Sound in Tacoma, Washington. My sister, Laurie, was living in Olympia, Washington and invited me to go to a metaphysics class which was being taught at a local school.

We attended the class where a woman channeled a being named "Jonah". Jonah had a very warm and humorous personality. He was quite blunt. He reminded me of a wise cracking, cigar smoking, poker player. He too was very uplifting and shared a lofty perspective which allowed the questioners to make sense of their conflicts.

Jonah took questions from the audience. I wanted very much to ask a question about John, who at the time was my boss, and later became my husband. But I was rather shy about asking the question in a room full of strangers. I hesitated too long, and Jonah eventually disappeared from the channeler. At the time he left her, I felt a huge rush of energy in my throat.

The following evening I was home alone, playing with the Ouija board. "Jonah" came on the board and said he could answer my question now. Since the Ouija board was limiting in developing a fluid conversation, he suggested we try automatic writing. (Automatic writing involves holding a pen to paper and allowing the spiritual entity to move the pen and communicate through writing.) That was somewhat productive, yet given my compulsion regarding wasting paper, I suggested we try voice channeling. Jonah told me to go look in the mirror. I did and saw myself. I interpreted that to mean that I could channel. I sat down on my bed and began a meditation. I had been practicing Transcendental Meditation twice daily since I was 16 years old, so I simply began a mental repetition of my mantra. Sure enough, I began to voice channel Jonah that night.

For the next 6 years, I channeled mostly as a form of entertainment for close friends. My mother originally thought I had developed schizophrenia to cope with the stress of law school. My father thought I was the best actress he had ever seen. I didn't tell many people that I channeled. Most of the people I did tell were not particularly interested. The practice pretty much remained in the closet until the summer of 1985.

I believe that nearly everyone has had "metaphysical" experiences. However, hardly anyone talks about them. Fear of being a kook, I guess. My sister-in-law, Robin O'Brien, had for some time been a believer in metaphysics. However, I didn't know that. One evening, though, over dinner with my father-in-law, she began to tell him about the Seth books. I about fell off my chair. "Robin, I channel," I exclaimed. Wow, support in the family. I was excited.

From that point forward, Robin encouraged me to channel. I didn't know anyone else who was interested. She did. Soon enough I was channeling for small groups of people in Seattle. I was amazed by their positive responses. I was happy to channel, simply to give others exposure to the phenomenon. For me, it provided the opportunity to have the energy of sheer love rush through my body. It gave me the deepest sense of relaxation I had ever known. Every criminal defense lawyer needs a healthy way to relax. The more I channeled, the better I felt.

Summer turned into fall. My meditation class provided more support for my channeling. In one meditation I visualized walking out on my lawyer job. The euphoria I felt was overwhelming. At that moment, I decided to see what it felt like in "real" life. I left my lawyer's job, with the security of another one waiting in the wings if I wanted it. I began to channel regularly for individuals, and Robin and I began the thrice weekly channeling sessions which became the chapters of this book.

During this time, I also began channeling "Raphael," a guide for those involved in the "light" energy meditation classes. Raphael defines herself as a vibrational form of consciousness. She insists, however, that every definition places a limit on potential, and therefore she does not like to be "placed in a box" through further definition. She exclaims that she is "all that is now, was, and ever will be." She insists that each of us is just as expansive in our own natures as well.

The consciousness of Raphael is genderless. However, to ease communication with myself and others, she adopts a persona, in this case female, when channeling through me. (My meditation teacher channels consciousness "of the same vibration" and it takes on a more male persona when channeled through him.) The "Raphael" that I channel speaks with an English-type accent. She is funny, nonjudgmental, upbeat, insightful, poetic and very loving.

My life transformed. I saw sunlight dance in my window and fall upon the chair at 10:00 o'clock in the morning. I could smell the aroma of pine when I walked outside at noon. I noticed the weather. I could listen to people when they talked to me. I began to feel emotions I had never felt. Life became ALIVE. I felt so good. For a time, I kept waiting for it to end, the crash to come. For the morning when I would have to drag myself out of bed at 5:00 a.m., and throw myself into the shower, to awaken me to prepare for a cross-examination of a rape victim. For the blood from the autopsy reports to come dripping back into my dreams. But instead the sky got bluer. I had high voltage love rushing through my body on an almost daily basis. The headaches went away. The muscle rocks dissolved. Could it be I had found the happy medium? The place where pleasure and pain become one? The place where every breath becomes an act of creation?

Many of the concepts in this channeled material may seem hard to accept. It is always difficult to accept responsibility for the creation of one's own life. Yet, when you acknowledge the power within that created your life—you accept the challenge of consciously creating every moment of your existence from this moment forward.

Acknowledgements

My belief is that I am a composite of all the people, places and things I have experienced in my life. I believe that every piece of writing is created by many different sources of energy. The words of this book have come to us from another dimension. I am the channel through which the words have come.

Taking the steps to become a public channel is one of the hardest things I have ever done. For me, channeling has always been as natural as breathing. To this day I have some trouble understanding why the very notion of channeling arouses such conflict in people. Yet now I know it does. Since going public with my channeling I have been called, among other things, a fake, a fraud, self-deluded, pathological, schizophrenic and the devil. Withstanding such hostile criticism takes a great deal of self-trust and courage. The main source of my strength comes from the God within me. Yet I also acknowledge it would have been so much harder without the love and support of my family and friends. Therefore, Thanksgiving is graciously extended to the following loved ones:

To Jonah and Raphael, for filling my life with richness and sensation. For guiding me as I transform. For loving me unconditionally, and for teaching me to believe in things I cannot see.

To my parents, for bringing me up to believe in myself, and for accepting my choices, unorthodox as they may have sometimes been. To my mother, Dottie, for raising me to have a heart that feels, a mind that questions, and a spirit that soars. To my father, Ron, for teaching me never to be intimidated, for allowing me to learn the value of different opinions, and for showing me that a man's strength lies in loving compassion. To his wife, Jill, for loving and supporting me in my uniqueness. To my grandmother, Edna, who teaches me every day that it is never too late to grow. To my sister, Laurie, for her loving spirit, for helping me to understand the beauty of simplicity, and for showing me that we all have more in common than we know. To my brother, Vance, whose life is a living dedication to principle. For his artistic expression, the glory of which will always inspire me. To my sister, Shauna, for teaching all of us to believe in miracles. For being a living example that the human will can overcome all physical obstacles. To my niece, Aya, for letting me see the world through the eyes of a child. For renewing my enthusiasm for things I once took for granted. To my new baby daughter, Kailani, for allowing me to experience a miracle first hand, for teaching me about emotional expression, trust, the power of the present and for opening my heart in ways I never dreamed possible.

To Robin, for encouraging me, for believing in me, and for touching parts of me that led me to have faith in my own dreams. For being a companion on this journey, and for living her life with such a vibrant belief in the principle contained within this book, that her example keeps my own life on track. To Lynn, for her loyal support in the earliest days of my channeling. For her courage in joining me out there on the limb. For her commitment to uplifting life on our planet and bringing *Voices of Light* to the world. For being my mirror, and a good one at that. And most importantly, for the intimacy and honesty that come from understanding me like no one else on earth. To Zsa, for growing up with me. To Mary, for asking me hard questions. For being a fellow seeker of the meaning of life. For showing me that the breadth of a womans love is fathomless. To Judy, for a loyal, provocative and steadfast friendship. For setting an example of maintaining beauty and depth of character in the midst of a professional climb. For sending me into orbit every time she touches the keys of a piano. To Karen, for sharing my old dream with an intimacy I longed for and treasured when I found. For keeping the torch aflame. To Lisa, for her freshness, and for keeping my political zeal alive. To Lori, for keeping me laughing. To Margaret, whose wisdom and humor have enabled me to understand myself on a deeper level. To Jeff, for staunch and loyal support during my days at the Defender. For continuing to be my friend as I grow and change. To Alexandra and Richard for being living examples of balance. To Geri for her zest for living. To Susan, Brad, Charmelle, Harvey, Jerry, Ed, Jeanette and High Spirits Farm for their loving support of my channeling.

To Paul, who turned me on to meditation at a tender age. To Jennings, for his love. For teaching me the light. To Kelly, for loving parts of me I did not see. To Emmanuel, for teaching me that love transcends language and culture.

To Freeman, for showing me my talent when I was a teenager. To Earl, for teaching me that all life is a matter of perspective. For riding the wind and swimming with dolphins. For writing and singing songs that celebrate the human spirit. For helping me believe in magic. To Len, for teaching me that every second counts. For turning me on to the pleasure of mundane tasks. For intensifying my understanding of the value of family. To Alan, for teaching me "economic" theory that changed my perspective on life. For demonstrating that even the hardcore can change. For sticking by me all these years.

To David Lanz, Danny Deardorff, and Michael Tomlinson, whose music opened up aspects of me that inspired me to go forward when I wanted to turn back.

To Kathryn Martin and my Wednesday Group, Michael Berni and my dear friends Daniel and Tim for joining me in the struggle to find our feelings.

To my agent Laura Meinhardt for her encouragement and zealous commitment to finding a publisher for my work. To Dawson Church and Brenda Plowman of Aslan Publishing for my first "call back" and their continued friendship. To Jim and Liz Gross of Uni ★ Sun for their dedication to publishing books which improve the quality of life on our planet. To Pat Huyett for her friendly and supportive editing. To Marilyn McGuire and Khit Adams for their enthusiastic promotional work. To Mark J. Adams for his beautiful cover art, the painting "Emerging". To Charmelle Pool for her fabulous photography.

To Karen and Robbie, whose magical fingers transformed the voices of Raphael and Jonah into written words.

To those who have criticized and condemned me. Your fears and insecurities often mirror my own.

To my channeling clients, for the courage it takes to look inward. For allowing me to share your journeys. For increasing the harmony on earth by working to increase the harmony in your own lives.

And most of all, to my husband, John, for having the patience of Job. For his unwavering support of my development. For training me as a lawyer, to stand tall in the face of seemingly insurmountable opposition. For teaching me to speak the words others were afraid to voice.

Acknowledgements

For sharing my tender compassion for the despicable and despised. For the strength it takes to make a commitment. And for loving me with such a passion that I came to believe I deserve it.

INTRODUCTION
The Beginning is the End

I greet you on this wondrous day.* This journey shall be written by those of us who desire to communicate with you upon the earth. We are desirous of continuing to be involved in your metamorphosis into the beautiful, enlightened beings you were meant to become. We are excited to once again have contact with those of you who are searching for spiritual and emotional enlightenment. We, as well, are endeavoring in our own daily activities to grow and progress spiritually. We are all brothers and sisters. We are all related. We are all connected by love. This book is a gift of love. It is an offering. It is a bounty.

This introduction is the beginning of the journey. It is also the end. This introduction begins and closes a gap in our communication.

There has been a void in the communication between those of us who have come together to write this

---

*This book was channeled by Jonah and Raphael. Occasional "guest appearances" were made by other entities as indicated. It is Jonah who greets us. Often during the dictations for this book Jonah and Raphael would merge their energies and speak as one. Spiritual beings, like human beings, are constantly growing and changing. They are very much aware of their interconnectedness with all other forms of life. Blending their energies in such a manner allows them to constantly recreate and expand who they are.

1

book, and those of you who have come together to listen and read. It is through the process of our communication that our love shall be expanded. We have come together to praise each other and to praise the God within each of us. This God is yearning to be set free. It is the setting free of the God within each of us that We are put here to accomplish. We shall free each other from the bondage of our restrictive ideas, the bondage of our physical dimensions. We shall take the form of change.

Through the coming together of human beings and spiritual entities, We shall find a love that has been lost. It is important that We understand at the beginning that there is a choice being made here. The choice is not only being made by those of us who find ourselves in a position of speaking the words which shall become the chapters of this book; the choice is also being made by those who have committed themselves to writing and reading these materials. The decision to produce these materials is being made for a common purpose. This choice has been made for the good of all humankind. The choice has been made consciously, and with full awareness of the results that shall come forth. The commitment to write and read these materials is an expression of love. It is important that We understand the commitment We are making to each other. These materials are an offering of prayer, for peace, prosperity and fulfillment for those living upon the earth.

The earth, in many of its moments seems to be terrorized by acts of destruction. The decision to produce these materials is therefore also made by the universe at large. The universe has found itself in a situation of conflict with the earth. The universe is in a pattern where it is seeking to unfold in a most enlightened and spiritual way. Yet the people of the earth, at times, seem resistant to this path. You disrespect the life of your planet by polluting your air and water. You cut your trees and blast your land without reverence for life. You kill yourselves and each other in the name of God. Disease runs rampant upon your plane. The threat of nuclear holocaust looms over you a like a black cloud. Many of you refuse to recognize that you are not alone in this universe.

And yet We hear your prayers. We hear you pray for peace. We hear you pray for health and prosperity. We see that you are opening your hearts, your minds and your eyes. These messages are answers to your prayers.

The conflict between the earth and the universal spiritual unfolding brings forth this information. Conflict is often the catalyst for peaceful growth. It is somehow inconsistent, and contradictory, that it should be through something negative that the positive shall come forth. However, it is precisely the potentially destructive path that the earth finds itself moving towards that brings human beings and non-physical spiritual beings closer together. This conflict draws us into each other's energy spheres, so that We may combine our efforts to imporve the quality of life on earth and in the universe at large. Let us begin day one of the journey.

The journey began a very, very long time ago. The journey began longer ago than your scientists can imagine in the smallness of the human mind. The journey began so long ago that it has not been recorded in history. Words do not exist within your language to define this period of time. The earth was not even in existence as a physical form at the time the journey began. But you were there. You do have a memory of this beginning. You know deep within your hearts and souls that you originate from a common source of energy. This energy is God.

Creation began as an explosive thought form. You call

this force light. This explosive force took the form of sparks, of fire. It is difficult to describe this concept to you because you are not familiar in your physical reality with this form of energy. This energy is malleable. This energy can take form, it can make creation, simply by manifesting thought. This was the beginning of consciousness as you know it.

Your physical earth was not around in the very beginning. Earth was an afterthought. In many ways Earth was a diversion. Earth was a split off from this ultimate form of consciousness. Earth became a lost loved one.

Due to this process of separation, you now find yourselves beginning to undertake the journey back home. The journey will lead you back into the hands of God. The journey will lead you to discover your own inner soul, your own inner essence, your own ability to become creative thought.

The beginning of this journey, is in fact the end of this journey. It is your beginnings that you long for. It is your beginnings that you are striving for. It is your beginnings, that you yearn for in the deepest crevices of your heart and soul. This journey will take you one step closer to finding this beginning. This journey will take you one step closer to heaven. It is a heaven where you will be most welcome. You shall find yourself comforted by all of those around you, whom you have longed for since you began this separation. There you shall find unconditional love. Competition, jealousy, and power struggles, shall no longer exist. It is heaven in the sense that it is the ultimate form of consciousness. It is the place that you long to be. You long to be there in the same sense that a child, once born, is always seeking, in some way, to go back to the womb. It is the place where you shall find your comfort. It is the place where you shall find your home.

Introduction: The Beginning Is The End

So my friends, as We set forth upon this journey together, let it be known that your beginning shall also be your end, and that your end my friends, shall also be your beginning. We embark upon this journey in an attempt to bring together the beginning, the middle, and the end.

The journey shall be a creative, rewarding experience. In many ways the journey may be a lonely experience. It may change the way you perceive your lives. It may change the way you perceive reality. It may change the way you think. It may change the way you experience relationships. It may change the basic structure of your life and the lives of those around you.

This change in the way you perceive things is necessary. It is meant to occur. If you should find these writings in your hand, come along, if only for the ride. The ride may be bumpy at times. It may be disconcerting to you. It may be fraught with tension and with question. Ultimately you make the choice as to whether or not to be involved in this journey. It is a necessary choice for each of you to make. In making this choice, each of you shall come a little closer to home.

This journey is being embarked upon by many people. This journey may be the beginning of monumental change in your life. When you embark upon this journey, be prepared. Prepare yourself in the same way you prepare for a physical journey. Think about your itinerary. Pack your bags. Take your own ideas, thoughts, and feelings with you. Take them along but do not be afraid to discard them, if you feel as though they are weighing you down. Plan for your life to be altered by this travel. Be flexible. Be prepared to make changes as you begin this journey. For this journey may shatter many of your preconceptions about the world. This journey may shatter many of your illusions about the nature of reality. It

5

will take you places you have never been before. So my friends, be sure to bring along the cameras of your soul. Bring along your journals. You may wish to review this journey in the same way you would review the slides of a physical trip that you have taken.

Remember where you have been as you embark upon this journey. Realize, as you travel through the mountains, the rivers, and the valleys of your soul, that you shall be confronted by those who are programed to confront or ignore you.

The journey shall not only be recorded by each of you on the physical plane, but it shall also be recorded by each of us on the spiritual plane. We shall be making this journey with you. We shall be recording it for our own posterity. We shall be your friends, your guidance counselors, and your traveling companions along the way.

You are left today to think on these things. Although this is the beginning, the beginning and the end are ultimately tied together. As We journey along it is important We not attempt to see too much at once. We must not fatigue ourselves. We must make this a peaceful, easy and yet most enlightening trip.

Part One:
Blast Off

You are God's Gift to Yourself

G od is the beginning and the end of all things. God
consciousness is the source from which all human
will is born. Each of you are surrounded by divine masters who seek to come to you to give you this reassur-
ance. They seek to awaken you to this depth of being.
They seek to plant within you the seeds to allow you to
spring forth into this enlightened state. They seek to give
you wisdom.

Wisdom is simply knowledge that is experienced. Wisdom is having an experiential base from which to discuss
actual data. Wisdom is essentially a process you shall go
through as you learn more about your inner being.

Wisdom has its birth and its death from the same
source. The stream from which all eternal beings come is
that stream of consciousness, that spring of divine will,
known to you as God's consciousness. This particular
form of consciousness is being made available to you
through these lessons. This consciousness is being made
available to you as you endeavor to understand metaphysical theory. This consciousness is not hard and fast.
There are not rules except that truth springs eternal.

The lessons can be used by all individuals in all walks
of life. The place where you walk in life and where you
find yourself this day, is the place where it is important

for you to be. The place where you are, the place from where you have come, and the place where you are going, is really one and the same.

The place you have come from and the place you are going to is that homeland which you have sought with every breath you breathe. The homeland you are looking for is that land of euphoric self-knowledge.

Know yourself. You have heard these words before. You have endeavored to understand what they mean. What does it mean to know yourself? To know yourself on the deepest level is to know God. To know God is to know yourself. You, my dear friends, are God. You are the life that God has given you. You are the song God has given you to sing and the dance God has given you to dance. You are energy which changes forms at different times in different places. You are the divine consciousness which you are seeking to know. What you seek outside of yourself can be found within your heart. Those things you imagine to be external to your being are really a part of all of creativity. You are a part of all of creativity. You, my dear one, exist outside of yourself. Although you perceive yourself to be separate and distinct from the outside world, you are not separate and distinct. You are indivisible.

Do not continue to view the world in a way which places a limit upon your own consciousness. Perceive yourself intimately connected with all energy which flows in and about you. Begin to perceive yourself as being fluid. Begin to perceive yourself as being intimately intertwined with all those around you. Those whom you view with hatred and hostility, you will come to know and understand as your beloved brothers and sisters. You shall begin to have an understanding of yourself as being God. Think of yourself as God. It is not your ego speaking when you perceive of yourself as having divine consciousness. It is not the big-headed person who believes he is God. It is the smallest and the most humble who allows himself to perceive that God is within him.

True power is not in personality, the size of the body, or the strength of muscles. True power lies in wisdom. Wisdom is simply to know God. We are all God. We are all creators of the reality we give God credit for creating.

How then can we allow ourselves to begin the process of actualizing what we accept as intellectual theory? We can begin in a simple way—by engaging in a very deep and loving act of trust. We must trust ourselves. Understand that your own lack of trust in the universe, yourself, and in God, is the act that brought you to this plane in the first place. Understand that your lack of trust in the purity of the essence, and the divinity of the unconscious is what created your separation from the original source in the first place.

Begin to put the pieces back together. Begin to solve the puzzle. Begin to view the world around you as fitting together in a beautiful and divine scheme. Trust in your ability to heal. Trust in your ability to repair the woes of the world. Trust in your ability to right the wrongs. Perceive that all that is happening is happening for a reason. Trust in your ability to search, and to find those reasons. Trust in your ability to move slowly and surely, step by step, day by day, back to that original place. That place where there were no fears. That place where trust and love were one and the same. That place where there is no trauma, terror, and turmoil. You shall find there is a garden gate open for you. The path leading from the garden is lined with flowers. The sun is shining down upon you from all angles. The road is as smooth or as bumpy as you would like it to be. It is not as though you are going to be lost in the Land of Oz. You shall actually be found in a place that makes more sense to you than you can possibly imagine. So open that garden gate my dears. Open that gate and set yourself free.

Freedom is yours for the asking. Inspiration is here for the taking. In those moments when you doubt yourself and lack belief in your own power, you shall have the opportunity to feel the surge of divine love and divine trust. These gifts are yours, but you need to open yourself to the gifts. The gifts cannot be considered gifts if there is no receiver. A gift is given by one unto another. You are the others who shall be receiving these gifts. In your reception you have returned the gift to the universe. For in the acceptance of the gift of divine love and power, you are accepting a gift which has far- reaching consequences. Divine love and power have the ability to transform the physical world into a euphoric and Utopian place.

The Man and Woman
Within You

Male and female energies are the key to many wondrous worlds of discovery. Within each of you these two forces are at work. It will be beneficial for you to learn how to create compatibility between these energies instead of allowing them to be warring factions. The male and female aspects of your being are embedded within your soul. You can draw upon either of these energies when their particular forces are beneficial for your situation.

Your culture has male and female roles. These roles have been more or less "socially ordained." However, the true ordination of male and female energy comes from the universal structure and flow of consciousness. You have simply developed the male and female bodies as a way of expressing these energies. These energies exist outside of the male and female bodies as well. They exist in places where the concepts of male and female are unknown.

Male and female energies are polarized. You express polarization by many concepts. East and West. Hot and Cold. Black and White. These concepts characterize the opposite extremes of particular energy forces in your universe. You use male and female role models as a way to express these particular kinds of energy. Recognize that these energies will remain with you long after you leave your male or female organs behind. They were a part of you long before you donned your male or female bodies.

These energies have a root which goes far beyond your male and female species—the root of consciousness. Originally, when consciousness was desiring a way of expressing itself, it determined that interaction was necessary for expression. Therefore it devised two forms of energy which were opposite in their extremes. A magnetic attraction was developed. These opposites were then drawn to each other to express their individual nature and desires. Through the process of attraction and coming together, a third form of energy was established. That third form of energy is androgyny. Androgyny has been overlooked as a unique and singular form of energy. You find it to have a fairly bland quality. Its true essence is the perfect combination of male and female energy. These opposites have discovered their common ground in androgyny.

Male and female energies are essential to productivity in your world. It is important that you begin to understand the energies and how you may use them in your daily life. The male energy has been given a fairly substantial lashing during the last two decades of your earth-plane existence. It has been criticized for its lack of passion in the way it experiences the world. One should not be so judgmental of this particular form of energy. It is crucial to your ability to understand the world in which you exist.

Male energy is associated with left brain consciousness. The male form of energy deals with programming. It makes your life plan. It is the organizer of your being. It is the side which is rational, intellectual, and interested in the mathematical calculation of life. It is the energy which you use on a conscious level to design your life's plan. You are actively using this energy when you set goals for yourself. Ambition and the desire to "climb the ladder" are attributes of male energy.

The male aspect of your being is forceful, strong and secure. Often people turn to their left brain conscious-ness to feel security. The male finds itself feeling most secure when it is dealing with the intellect, the left brain consciousness. The security your left brain will give you, however, will not last long. In your physical world it may reassure you, because the world in which you exist is essentially a left brain world. That is why the male humans on your planet have traditionally been the most powerful. Because your world is physical, it is a left brain, male energy world.

As the New Age sets itself upon you, you have begun to see a shift in this power structure. You have seen the advent and rise of feminism. You have an intellectual understanding of the rise of feminism. Yet the rise of feminism has its root in spirituality. The rise in feminism coincides with the rise of New Age consciousness. This is because the consciousness of the New Age is essentially a female energy consciousness.

Often you have wondered why those who are attracted to the metaphysical realm are the females, gay males, and the sensitized straight male population. Those individ-uals who are attracted to the metaphysical field are those open to their right brain consciousness. This is one reason why many traditional men are reluctant to accept metaphysical theory. They remain extremely skeptical because they are petrified of developing their right brain consciousness. They fear their female side. They view acceptance of metaphysical phenomenon as acceptance of female energy. They resist this energy because it makes them uncomfortable and insecure. To accept the right brain, or female energy, they must accept and rely upon faculties such as emotions, creativity and intuition. Men have always had a very difficult time in this area.

The female energy is the energy of the New Age, the energy of the future, and the energy of the generations to come. Children being born at this time on your earth are being born with more right brain-female energy. This is caused be the rise and acceptance of feminism and female power.

Women who are successful in the world today may seem to be more like men. Women who are succeeding in the business and corporate world appear to be operating out of their left brain hemisphere. This is simply a mirage. They portray an "image" to be successful in the "man's world." They are truly experiencing the world out of a right brain consciousness, but expressing themselves out of a left brain consciousness. Danger lies here. The woman of today is creating an almost schizophrenic-like process. She experiences the world in one way, yet expresses the experience in a different way. Experience is the first step. Expression comes next. Acceptance of female energy is a seeming prelude to its free and open expression.

Life is a step-by-step process. The first step has been to experience the female energy, yet express it through male concepts. The next step will be expressing female experience through right brain consciousness. Feminism and spirituality walk hand in hand.

All individuals have within themselves both male and female energy. They can tap into these energies and use them in situations where it is most productive. Some situations warrant the use of male energy, some warrant the use of female energy. The blending of these energies is the wave of the future.

Q: *How can we help the hard-core rational thinkers to be more open to New Age philosophy?**

A: Your question is of good concern. It is your desire to increase the knowingness of individuals on your plane. You perceive that by their increased understanding and acceptance of metaphysical belief, your world will prosper. However, what you believe is *your* truth. It works for you. It makes sense for you. Other individuals are not at a place in their evolutionary process where they are ready, open and willing to accept such beliefs. Your desire to aid them along in this process shows good intent, but it is not your role to lead them. They are the leaders of their own lives. At some point they shall come to an understanding of these beliefs. They must work through their own processes and come to their own understanding.

---

*The questions following the chapters were asked by actress/playwright Robin O'Brien. Robin was present at each channeling session and recorded the channeled information on a tape recorder. Occasionally other interested persons were present at the sessions. It was a good opportunity for people to experience the phenomenon of channeling without the "threat" that sometimes comes from channeling with regard to one's own personal issues.

Each dictation averaged about twenty minutes in length. I would simply bow my head, become very relaxed, set my consciousness aside, and allow the loving energy of Jonah and Raphael to "speak" through me. When I channel I hear the words that are spoken, but they float by me in a "stream of consciousness" type manner. I feel the emotional content of the material quite intensely. Coming out of the channeling process is very much like awakening from the dream state. I remember some, but not all of what took place.

The primary blockage to experiencing this understanding is fear of the unknown. They fear the right brain is unstable. They are uncomfortable with their feelings. It is much more difficult to control feelings. You can control your mind, and you can control your thoughts. Often you cannot control the way you feel. The lack of control frightens them.

The best way to share or express your beliefs is to set a good and strong example. Allow others to see the benefits you gain from expressing your feelings in your own life. Allow them to see what they are missing when they deny the feeling aspect of their being. If you can express your emotions in ways that appear desirable, others will want to follow suit.

It is the negative aspects of emotionalism which have been played up in your culture. You need to play up and express the more wondrous side of emotions. You express this in relationships between lovers. However, you need to begin expressing the emotions you feel about everything in life. The feelings you have towards work, nature and politics all have tremendous emotional aspects. It is the emotional aspects of thought that give concepts their power. Every successful politician is able to arouse the emotions in people. Truly successful individuals figure out how to evoke emotions. You see it in your television commercials. The most successful commercials are those evoking emotion. You see it in your courtrooms. Successful attorneys are the ones who are able to evoke emotions. So if individuals can perceive that the evocation of emotions gives them power, instead of taking it away, they may be more apt to develop this side.

Beyond the Material "Girl"

E ach of you has a variety of personalities within your soul. A multi-faceted variety of life exists within each of you. It is important that you begin to discover the aspects of yourself which inhabit your inner being. In learning about these various aspects of yourself, you will have the opportunity to develop and express them. Through the process of discovering the various beings which exist within you, you shall have the opportunity to express your creativity, your intellect, your mind, your emotions and your physical nature. Within each of you there are aspects of being lying dormant. Each of you has talents which are not being developed. Within each of you there is a spark of consciousness desiring to express itself in your world.

The discovery begins in a discussion of the left brain/-right brain form of consciousness. Many of you are familiar with this concept. The left brain is that side of yourself which has been denoted as masculine. It is the rational, intellectual, logical side of your being. Your right brain is the more feminine side, the creative side, the side of emotion, intuition, and creative expression. The brain is grossly underdeveloped in most human beings. The left brain is important to you, but tends to overshadow the right brain consciousness. The right and left brain are engaged in an ongoing battle for power. The aim should be to develop the right brain, so that it will complement the left brain.

SOJOURNS OF THE SOUL

There is ample opportunity to develop right brain consciousness. The opportunity greets you in every day you exist. However, you cling steadfastly to your left brain consciousness, because it gives you security in your material world. In order for you to develop your right brain consciousness, you must begin to release your hold on the material world. In your time there has been a tremendous focus on material goods and possessions. Your hit songs extol the virtues of living in a material world. It is good of you to take cognizance of the materiality of your existence. It will be even better of you to release this consciousness, so that you are not bogged down and imprisoned by your material world.

Material goods and possessions are essential to your existence on the physical plane. However, they are essential only because you believe they are essential. You believe that it is important for you to have furniture, housing, clothing and food. Yet you have gone beyond the mere necessities, and developed a lustful desire for fine perfume, clothing, jewelry, and expensive stereo equipment. You have an utter fascination with toys . . . cars, boats, motorcycles and such. These things are important to you because of your left brain consciousness. Your left brain relies upon physical reality for its reinforcement. Your left brain relies upon being able to have possessions which one can "touch" in a physical sense. Left brain consciousness is reinforced by material possessions. The more material possessions you acquire, the more you are affirming your left brain consciousness. The left brain has the desire to acquire. This desire gives evidence of the emptiness and insecurity existing in your life on the physical realm. Material possessions are often used as a gauge of success in the material world. Your left brain insists upon having what is physical to reinforce its logic.

20

It is necessary for you to have left brain consciousness in your reality. However, it is increasingly necessary for you to be able to release left brain aspects, so room can be made for the more creative, intuitive side of your being to surface.

It is fine to relish and take pleasure in your physical possessions. You live in a physical world. Love your physical world. Find sensuous pleasure in food, music, perfume, and in all other aspects of your physical life. Yet, begin to perceive of the material things in which you find pleasure, as sources of energy. The pleasure you are finding in these physical objects is not pleasure which is being derived from the physical nature of those possessions. What you are truly experiencing, loving and enjoying from your material success, is the "energy" which it gives to you.

Food is the ultimate example. You can spend tremendous physical resources on attaining a scrumptious and delightful meal. You do not necessarily find pleasure in the "physicalness" of the meal. You exchange the "energy" of money for the "energy" and pleasure of food. Recognize that everything you ingest in your physical body is an energy. You will find confirmation of this from your nutritionists. Food has always been perceived of as energy. So attribute energy to your food.

Another example is music. When you purchase stereo equipment, or musical albums, you do not derive your pleasure simply from the acquisition. Music is a wondrous source of energy. The expenditure of finances brings back to you the marvelous feelings and emotions that music can evoke. Recognize as well, that your clothing and perfumes are not merely physical objects. They are expressions of who you are. They are expressions of your inner creative self. Perfume and clothing can evoke tremendous fantasy and emotion.

The things that you acquire and term material and physical, are really only symbols for the energy you create. What you really purchase is not an object to touch. What you buy is an object that will fill you with wondrous feelings.

Your right brain consciousness can be activated with the snap of your fingers. It is important that you begin the process of opening up that consciousness. You can do this by giving the right brain permission to open up and become a receptor to information and knowledge. It is the right brain consciousness which acts as the filter and interpreter for all channeled material. It is right brain consciousness which will give you the flow necessary for your written and artistic endeavors.

Envision your right brain opening up, much as a flower would open up to receive the energy of the sun. Envision a beautiful flooding of radiant white and gold energy into your right brain consciousness. You may visually attempt this in your meditations. You shall then begin to experience more right brain activity.

Your right brain has always taken a back seat to your left brain. But your left brain is really tired of steering and having to follow directions. Your left brain is ready to allow your right brain to take over and begin to direct the journey. In your own brain/mind consciousness, thank and bless your left brain for its continued existence. Now, allow your right brain to surface, and to channel a new direction. The left brain and right brain are companions along this journey. They have come together for you to experience cohesive action. They will continue to merge at your direction. They can merge into a "one brain consciousness" where they can co-exist together, ebbing and flowing, allowing the intellect and the creative emotion to co-mingle in a most productive way.

Q: *I'm trying to let go of the idea that having possessions makes a person non-spiritual. It seems to me that by saying the material world makes one more involved with the logical left brain, you are saying one doesn't want possessions if she wants to be spiritual.*

A: I do not mean to say that having possessions means one is non-spiritual. What I mean to say is that your possessions should be perceived of as energy forms, and that your acquisition of them is acquisition of energy, as opposed to mere acquisition of the material object. It is wonderful and joyous to possess what your physical universe has to offer you. However, do not only possess it—love it, and be sensitive to the energy which it is bringing to you.

Take a Ride on Your Emotions

Your philosophy determines what you think about life, death, and life beyond death. Philosophy is the field that attempts to look at reality. Each of you turn to it when you endeavor to seek the truth. It gives you your belief system and structures the way you observe the world. Philosophy gives you the opportunity to learn what is not yet known. It gives you the opportunity to think about life beyond your present physical realm.

Turn to the field of philosophy to understand the journey of the human soul. Your philosophy has attempted to define its origin for you. Philosophy gives you the opportunity to look inside yourself. It gives you the key to understanding human reality.

Philosophy however, has also been your limit and your barrier. Your philosophy is not only what you think, but what you permit yourself to see. Your philosophy frames your thought, and defines your belief system. Your philosophy is really only a way to limit your concept of reality. Strict adherence to a particular philosophy does not allow you to expand your consciousness. By putting concepts into rigid definitions, you destroy the opportunity to look beyond them. By looking beyond these definitions, you shall discover your freedom and the birthplace of your soul.

SOJOURNS OF THE SOUL

Your soul had its origin long ago. Your soul was birthed as a direct part of the source. It split from the source many light years ago, and descended into physical reality. Fear and mistrust developed. A disharmonic state evolved between your soul and the original source. Your soul then descended into its physical reality where it has been fearful and limited, yet struggling with hope to go back to its original source. The field of philosophy offers you a ride.

Philosophy gives you the opportunity to open the door, step out into the heavens, into the stars, and to pass through the gates to find home. Philosophy gives you the opportunity to think about the journey home. Thinking is a wonderful way to travel. When you think about philosophy, you think about the world beyond. You think about what you cannot hear, what you cannot see, and what you cannot touch with your fingers and your hands. Give birth to the notion that you can touch with a part of you which is not your hand—that you can touch with your heart, your soul, and your emotional strength. Philosophy gives power to those things which cannot be seen.

Your emotions cannot be seen. Your emotions have tremendous power and strength. In many ways they guide you as you walk upon the earth. Your emotions allow you to feel those things that cannot be verified in scientific ways. Your emotions allow you to come in contact with a tremendous source of energy—the love exuding from your heart and soul.

Take a ride on your emotions. Let yourself feel. Let yourself go. Your emotions stem from the part of you which is in touch with the greater universe, that part of you which is raw, virgin and vulnerable at its core. Your emotions stem from the place which is connected.

You are constantly analyzing and intellectualizing your emotions. But they need not be so analyzed. Your emotions are a very pure and real communication when they are not filtered by your thinking process. They are a string, an umbilical cord, which keeps you tied to the original source of all being.

You question your negative emotions. You wonder about the emotions of anger, pain, rage, jealousy, and insecurity. You are concerned about the conflict they create. How can these negative emotions be connected to a source which is all-giving, all-loving, divine? These emotions too, are propelled by a positive force. However, they are misused, abused and mistreated by your perception of them. You allow your intellect to run them over and define them. Emotions which you perceive to be negative are messages from your inner self. Your being is trying to escape from repression. Your being desires to live on the lighter side of love and light. The emotions you perceive to be negative are the truest forms of communication. They are urging you to change something in your life. They are urging you to redefine the way you think about reality. They are urging you to go forward.

When you experience emotions such as anger and rage, it is important that you stop, look and listen. When you experience these "negative" emotions you are listening to your heart talk. Your heart is telling you it is time to redefine the way you think. It is time to change the way you act.

All emotions are your teachers. This is true whether they bring laughter and joy, or tears and sorrow. Your emotions are your guides. They are communications from the part of yourself you are separated from. Emotions are attempts to call your attention to certain matters, things that need a shuffling around in your life.

Emotions should not be covered up. They should not be buried from your consciousness. They should not be turned away. When emotions come knocking at your door, they are begging for your attention. Listen to them. Allow them to guide you.

Your emotions are your loved ones. They have the capacity to bring you tremendous joy. Your emotions are a vibrant form of human energy. Your emotional energy has yet to be harnessed and used for the constructive good of each of you. Your emotions are ready, willing and able to take you for a very swift ride into the next dimension. Take a ride on your emotions.

In many ways, each of you uses your emotions as another divisive factor to keep you a little farther away from home. You use your emotions to create chaos, conflict, turmoil, and to barricade yourself from the ultimate connection with your soul. You use them to confuse yourself, and to prevent you from seeing the true issue. Begin the process of integrating your emotions into your very being.

This process of integration will allow you to move and flow as one force, instead of numerous separate forces. You have separated your emotions from your intellect, your intellect from your physical body and your mental process from your emotions. It's important that you begin the process of integrating these various processes. Begin to define yourself as one whole being, emanating many beautiful, positive, and forceful characteristics. Flow forward with a sense of divinity. Seek to make whole that which has been divided. Come together within yourself. Your philosophy has given you the seeds from which you could begin to comprehend the universe. It has also been a limiting force. Your philosophy has allowed you to intellectualize your emotions. It has allowed you to use your mental processes to separate

28

what you know from what you feel. This is an exercise in alienation. It is an exercise in futility. It will lead you farther away from your home. Your home will be one step closer, if you begin to actively make an attempt to integrate your emotional self with the rest of your being.

Q: *If we are not to intellectualize our emotions, how can we integrate our intellect and our emotions?*

A: Your emotions should not be defined as a separate form of consciousness from your intellectual concepts. Your intellect defines your emotions. It is equally important that your emotions define your intellect. Begin to practice defining your intellect by your emotions. In other words, feel your intellectual thoughts, instead of intellectualizing your emotional thoughts. There tends to be a separation between what one feels and what one understands on the intellectual level. I encourage you to take your emotions and use them to feel your thoughts. You will be emoting and feeling what you would normally use your brain to define. In other words, your emotions can become your thinking process. Your emotions and your thoughts shall become one form of energy instead of two—two which are normally seeking to battle each other. Does that make any sense to you?

Q: *Yes, I think that's clear.*

A: It's a difficult concept to understand because people are not used to feeling what they think. They're normally used to thinking about what they feel, instead of feeling what they think. Bring these processes together so that the form of communication will be more powerful and more pure.

Individuality: Fear of Surrender

The subject of individuality is of concern to each and every one of you. Individuality has its strong points. However, an obsession with maintaining it is in many ways a fear of surrendering oneself to the original source. Your attachment to your "identity" is one means by which you reinforce your separation from God.

Your individuality is part and parcel of a greater scheme. It fits into the collective consciousness. That is what makes your individuality a comforting place for you. Your individuality is your home.

Your individuality is not formed by you alone. It has been molded by, and is growing through, its interactions with those around you. Your individuality is really a product of the collective consciousness. In seeking interaction with others, you are able to define and understand your own individuality better. You are able to seek a broader perspective on what that individuality is.

Individuality is a combination of numerous different egos. Your ego structure has many different compartments. It consists of your personality being, your physical being, your mental processes, your emotions, and your spiritual nature. All these aspects have a separate function to perform. These aspects of your being interrelate to create your identity. Your identity is the collec-

31

tive consciousness of your body, mind and spirit. As you move forward in the twentieth century, your individuality and ego structures are going to be undergoing monumental change. Through these changes, you are going to need a broader perspective than that which you have allowed yourself to hold. You are going to be traveling faster and faster as you approach the next century. As you go through this experience, the vibrational structure of the earth is going to increase. Your thoughts are going to be transmitted in a much faster way. Your thought patterns will have more power. As you progress into this new vibrational state, your thoughts will carry the power to manifest your own reality.

When you begin the process of being able to create by your thoughts, it will be important to surrender your ego identity to a power which is greater than your lower ego self. In this surrender, there shall not be the loss of individuality. There will not be the loss of power, or the weakening of your individual will. In this surrender, you are simply letting down your defenses. You are letting go of fear and allowing yourself to open up to divine energy.

Through this experience, you will have the opportunity to make the connection with your higher self and the original form of consciousness. The connection will be made in your moments of quiet solitude.

As you struggle for this connection, you will recognize that there are parts of yourself which need to be released. Those aspects of yourself which are being released are not being released permanently; they are momentarily being set aside to make room for others. You are letting go so that there will be room for other thoughts, other ego structures, other ideas. They need space to present themselves.

It is your fear which needs to be set aside. Your fears

are intimately involved with your egos. In the back of your mind, the voice of fear will always want to keep you back. The voice wants to keep you strapped in your safety belt.

When you are able to hear your fears, you have the great opportunity to release them. Recognize them and you have the opportunity to grow. In growing you go forward on your path.

Your individuality is your most loved friend. In many ways it can be your most loved limitation. Allow your ego structures the opportunity to glide into the sky for a moment of time. Let them look themselves over, love themselves, understand themselves, and let go of themselves. In this surrender you come a little closer to home.

Q: *Do you have exercises that you can give people to help them surrender their fears?*

A: Fear is the blockage which makes it difficult to go forward. There are many ways in which you can begin to surrender your fears. Be patient, for this process is slow. It takes courage and a tremendous amount of support.

To start you must have faith. You must trust and believe in yourself. You are the foundation which exists beneath you, above you, and around you. You envelope yourself. The beloved self which you behold is all powerful, all loving, and has the energy to sustain you in times of crisis. You must recognize and tap into your inner powers. In order to do that, you need to understand and trust yourself. Believe in yourself. Practice self trust everyday.

You are going to make choices. You must have faith in your choices. You must believe in your choices. Go into your choices with a sense of commitment. There are no wrong choices, only opportunites to grow. You need to tell yourself over and over again as you go through your daily existence, that you are worth listening to. You are worth listening to because you are connected to the divine source. You can trust that source, so you can trust yourself. Learning to trust yourself is the most important lesson there is to learn. It is easier said than done. You need to start believing in yourself. To do this, you must actively think positively and lovingly towards yourself. Do not berate yourself. Do not put yourself down.

Begin this process by affirming yourself in daily meditations. Seek in every way that you live to perceive of yourself as divine consciousness. Tell yourself over and over again how beautiful you are, how loving you are, and how trustworthy you are. If you don't believe it yourself, no one else will either. That is the beginning. Love yourself.

Patterns are Made to be Broken

There are moments in our lives when we lose our judgment. Are there benefits to these periods in our lives? Are there benefits to acting in ways which seem to create destruction in our personal lives? The answer is yes. The periods in your life when you make "bad" judgments are important. They are important because they create a situation from which you can learn. They also create an opportunity for the people around you to learn.

You do not seem to learn from the mistakes of others. Lessons, for some reason, need to be learned through your own activity. Recognize that the people around you are there to learn from also. The mistakes of others are your own mistakes. When you observe others engaging in behavior which is seemingly destructive, it is an opportunity for you to learn. Perhaps you can avoid that particular experience yourself.

You may feel as though these words are common knowledge. Yet, by your continued behavior on this plane, it is obvious to those of us in another dimension, that you are not learning from the mistakes which are made by your brothers and sisters. This is obvious by your history books, and by observing each of you in your personal lives.

How then can you find a fruitful learning experience

from the lessons of others? How can you begin to integrate into your own life, the lessons of others, when you are having a difficult time comprehending your own lessons? Recognize that if you are feeling affected by the behavior of another, you have been drawn into that person's experience, and there is a reason for your presence there. Your presence may give you an opportunity to vicariously experience the other individual's lesson, and therefore, vicariously experience for yourself the other person's growth.

Each action an individual takes has a rippling effect. In essence, everything one says or does has a reaction somewhere in the universe. If you are feeling the brunt of somebody else's actions, it is important for you to make a determination as to what your reaction to that should be. Each of you has control over your reactions. You have control over the way you perceive an event and how you shall respond. If an individual engages in behavior that is harmful to you, you have several choices as to how you can respond. You can become filled with anger and you can act out of rage. You can become filled with pain and agony and you can inhibit yourself from expressing a reaction. You can become hurt to the point where you shut down. Remember, you are experiencing that particular pain for a reason. You should be conscious of, and devise your reactions, with a sense of divine consciousness. You should thank the individual who is engaging in the harmful conduct for allowing you to learn the lessons from this particular experience. The rippling effect that you feel is directed at you for a reason.

Begin to develop an understanding of the reasons underlying particular behavior patterns. There are moments when behavioral patterns seem embedded in stone. There are some people who have been engaging in conduct for such a long time that to break free seems impossible. Impossibility is simply the greatest form of challenge. Impossibility is a beckoning to those of you who are ready to move mountains. Impossibility is a figment of the conscious mind. It is the intellectual rejection of the expansion of consciousness.

Your consciousness is desirous of learning and understanding the impetus behind certain behavioral patterns. There are those who seek to aid you in understanding the behavior of yourself or others. These guides shall come to you in your dream state and seek to communicate with you.

It is not impossible to understand and conquer your behavioral patterns. Patterns are established with the goal that they shall at some point, be disturbed. Patterns are made to be broken.

Begin to understand the rippling effects of your own behavior. When you think a thought, that thought carries with it the negative or positive vibrations that surround it. Energy follows thought. Thought is energy. You have power that you are not aware of. You have power that you cannot see. So if you are engaging in negative thinking patterns, you are creating for yourself those negative experiences which shall follow from the thought patterns. If you are desirous of changing a negative pattern in your life, begin simply by changing the way you think. For action often follows thought. By changing the way you think, you begin to change the way you act.

Acting by many people is done on a level which borders on the unconscious. Many individuals do not think before they act. Yet, on one level of their being they are "thinking" or they could not act. The thinking, however, has taken on a monotonous, robot-like pattern, so they appear to be acting without thinking. These "unconscious" patterns, in particular, are the ones that need to be broken. All action should be divine action.

Begin to practice what you preach. Begin to honor the concept that energy follows thought. Change your behavior by changing the way you think.

Q: *What place does anger have in expression?*

A: Anger is the soul crying out. It is the frustrations of the soul, saying, "I am not whole by myself. I am alone. I am not fulfilled." Anger is directed at another individual for one's own failure to forgive one's own soul for being unfulfilled. It is only because each of you perceive yourselves as being separate and distinct from one another that you can even conjure up the feeling of anger towards someone else. When you are angry, you are angry at yourself for being in a situation where you depend upon another for those needs which should be fulfilled by your own divine consciousness. When you express anger towards another, you are continuing to maintain and to further develop the separation that you imagine exists between physical bodies and individual souls. You are pushing away that which you desire to draw closer unto yourself.

The expression of anger is a way of protecting one's own soul from the infiltration of that of another. The expression of anger can serve to facilitate division. Learn from your anger. Learn from the anger of others. Recognize that the action engaged in by one individual which serves to anger another is simply a striving to develop each individual's consciousness.

Problems as Puzzles

An angle is a perspective. If you put two angles together, you have a triangle. Two angles joined together creates three angles. This is the angular way of thinking. The angular way of thinking entails being able to observe a phenomenon from one, two and three different perspectives. It allows you to perceive of the world as being holistic in nature. Perceive of the world as a puzzle in which all of the pieces fit together in a divinely created scheme. You are a part of that scheme. Discover the part that you have to play. Part of the discovery is pursuing problem solving with gusto and glory.

All of you have problems in your lives. Some of you thrive on problems. Some of you view your problems as challenges. Many of you could not function if you did not awaken each day with a problem to solve. You must come to recognize why you are creating problems in your life. To begin you must understand that you are the creator of your problems. Therefore you can also be the one who comes up with the solutions. This is a very simple thought, yet many of you do not seem to grasp it. You create the problems; you can solve the problems.

There are three levels on which you should analyze the problems you are facing in your life. The first level is the conscious level. The problem will come to you at some point in a very concrete way. You will recognize that you have a problem. It will create some kind of blockage in your life. This is the conscious level. You are able to actually see the problem. Being conscious of your problem is the first step towards developing a resolution. Being conscious of your problem is the first step in confronting the fear which is generally underlying the issue. Be conscious. Be open, honest, direct and concrete. Recognize your problem and confront it head on. It might be important for you to articulate your problem to others. You can articulate it to yourself by formulating it into writing.

The second level on which you must deal with your problems is the unconscious level. It is more difficult to perceive on this level because you are generally out of touch with your unconscious motivations and desires. The intent of this chapter is to allow you to enable yourself to become more in touch with the unconscious aspects of your being. Your unconscious mind exists within your brain, your heart, and your soul. Your unconscious mind is desirous of communicating and expressing itself to you. Your unconscious mind is the direct motivator of most of your behavior.

Begin the process of allowing your unconscious to surface. Observe the *effect* of your behavior. Examine the effect the problem has created. Sit down and really attempt to analyze this problem. What are the ways in which it is affecting your life? What is it preventing from occurring? Who are the other people who are involved in the process? What are the greater issues that are being affected by the problem? When you discover the effect that a particular problem is creating in your life, you will come in touch with the unconscious aspects of the problem. You will come in touch with your unconscious motivations and desires. In your conscious awareness, you may believe that the problem is not something that you would ever intentionally create. Yet when you look upon the problem from the perspective of the unconscious, you may recognize your needs, desires and fears are being expressed and manifested.

The third level on which you should observe and understand your problem, is the level where the conscious and the unconscious combine to work. Normally, they combine to work against you. It is our goal to enable you to use your conscious and unconscious to work *for* you.

First you must recognize the problem. Secondly, you must recognize the reason you have created it. You must recognize the effects that it has on others around you. You are then able to reverse the problem. The "problem" will then be able to benefit instead of impede you in life. You need to determine what you desire the effect to be.

Take the negative effects that have been created and reverse them into positive effects. The effect that you desire to create must become a conscious thought. This conscious thought will have the effect of reversing the unconscious thought that is creating the negative effect. Begin the process of reversing all of the negative effects. Begin this process consciously and with immediacy. Meditate upon the reversal of the negative effects. In the process of meditation, you allow yourself to get closer in touch with the unconscious aspects of your being. You allow your conscious thoughts to filter into your subconscious thoughts, thus reversing the negative subconscious programming. The subconscious thoughts then reverse themselves and are channeled into the conscious mind. The thoughts then have more power.

This particular method of solving problems can be very useful if you actively engage in it with sincerity and trust. It is important that you trust the process to work.

The power of trust and belief are essential in creative problem solving. You are the masters of your own destiny. You have the choice of whether to be thwarted or benefitted by your problems. In solving specific problems, you have the opportunity to create a marvelous form of energy reversal. You can treat the universe to a positive transformation.

Q: *There is a seminar that I would like to go to. I don't have the money yet. My problem is that I don't have enough money to go to this. How can I meditate on reversing the fact that I don't have enough money?*

A: Initially, you must understand that you have not exactly recognized the problem. The problem which is preventing you from going is not solely the fact that you do not have the money to go. You have the money to go if you want to go. The money is not really the problem. It is important that you try to recognize exactly what the problem is. The real problem is the priorities and values which exist in your present relationship. The blockage from allowing you to go is not so much the money. It is the effect of making the decision that you want to go, that you need to go, that it is important for you to go, and then impressing this on your partner. The problem is essentially a difference in values between where, how and when money should be spent in your relationship. You do not feel that you have as much power over spending the money, especially on things which you view as benefitting yourself. It is essential that your partner begin to realize that the expenditure of the money is really a benefit to the relationship as a whole. Recognize that the problem is not exactly the lack of money, but a dispute between you and your partner over where resources should be spent.

Q: *Perhaps what I should do is meditate on having the relationship come to a point where we can communicate these ideas?*

A: The first step is a recognition that the problem is not simply a problem of money. Then you must determine the effect that the problem is having. The effect that the problem is having is that it is making you feel powerless. It is making you feel powerless in your relationship, and in your ability to manifest for yourself those things that you want. Why is it that you have a need to feel powerless in this relationship? Why is it that you feel that the labor you engage in on a daily basis is somehow less deserving of the income which is coming into your household? Why do you feel these particular things? What you are really needing to strive for is a sense of equality in the relationship, regardless of whose paycheck brings in more income.

When you have determined the effect that this is having upon your relationship, then you need to begin the process of meditating to reverse that effect. Begin the process of meditating to view yourself as an equal earner of the income in your family. View yourself as having equal power over the dissemination of that income. Recognize that the work that you are performing is work which is bringing in at least half of the income. You are earning your share of that money. When you meditate upon this, you will recognize yourself as being powerful. When you perceive of yourself in this way, you would not view the expenditure of money on a seminar, as being frivolous, extravagant or unnecessary. You would begin to view it as a further step in your career. Recognize that your metaphysical and spiritual values are co-creators of your career. The money would be invested in the strengthening and burgeoning of your career. Begin the process of empowering yourself. Recognize yourself as a wage earner. Recognize the value of the seminar you want to attend. If you portray it this way to your partner, it would not be viewed as a waste of money. The problem is not so much that you do not have the money, but that you do not feel that you have an equal voice in how the money is spent.

Rapids and Stillpools: The Pacing of Spiritual Growth

R apids carry swirling water over the tops of rocks, and move it into a new existence. Spiritual growth sometimes moves like a rapid. At other times it occurs in a stillpool.

There are times in your life when you believe you are experiencing spiritual growth at a very slow rate. You desire to speed up the process and move along. This lesson is on learning to pace yourself. Pacing is extremely important in the development of the spirit. When you feel as though you are not going anywhere, not advancing rapidly enough, you are in fact actually growing in the time of stillness.

Stillness is extremely important. In the stillness there comes a time for reflection. In stillness there comes time for pondering. In the stillness you are given the opportunity to look into the water and see yourself. In other words, when the water is moving rapidly and swirling around you, you do not have the opportunity for self-reflection. Self-reflection is as essential to spiritual growth as rapid movement.

The times during which you experience rapid spiritual change are not particularly the most valuable times. It is important that a distinction be made between the sensationalism of experiencing metaphysical phenomenon and true spiritual growth. Often individuals believe that if they experience an astral projection, a channeling of sorts, or a psychic vision, that they are somehow growing in the spiritual realm. Of course this is growth of some sort. It is not, however, the growth that should be focused upon. Nor is it growth which should necessarily be sought. It is not the growth of the utmost importance. These methods are only tools. Experiencing such phenomena itself is not necessarily reflective of one's spiritual status. The phenomena of channeling, of astral projection and of psychic vision are only tools to help you become more self-aware. The tools may be useful, but the tools can also be used to avoid the real lessons which need to be learned.

Often the real lessons are to be learned in the moments of quiet solitude. Do not seek only to find exhilaration and excitement in your spiritual quests. Seek as well to find calm and serene moments, when you can think and reflect upon the true lessons you are to learn.

The true lessons of life are simple. The true lessons of life may seem ordinary. The way the sun casts a shadow may hold meaning for you. The number of flowers in your garden may be significant. The time your clock stops may have some relevance to your life. So pay attention to the world around you. Pay attention to everything which exists and make an attempt to understand it. What may appear to be obvious may be a lesson needing to be learned.

It is important as well, however, to have those moments of rapid change in your life. For in the moments of rapid change you may become connected, and be able to feel the earth's powerful movement. In the moments of rapid change, you may find that your hopes, desires and beliefs are affirmed. Rapid change may give you validation of your spiritual beliefs.

The validation that you seek outside of yourself may work for you to counteract your innate skepticism. Such external validation may help you to explain your thoughts to others. Yet true validation does not come from a being who speaks to you from an external plane. True validation comes from opening up, and receiving spirit into your heart. You need not reach outside yourself to find it. It is within your very heart, your very soul and your very body. It is there that the confirmation of spirit lies.

Q: *Today I noticed the fence. Everywhere I would look, I could see the movement of things, holding themselves together. It only happened for awhile. Why is it that something like that is hard to maintain?*

A: Your question raises a good point. You are in fact grounded in a physical reality. You need to function in this particular reality. It is not essential that you maintain that kind of perception for a long period of time. It is not essential that you continually view the world as you were able to view it for a moment in time this morning. It is important that you begin, however, to have an understanding that that is how the world operates. Perceive that there is this continuous movement and this continuous energy. Be understanding of the knowledge. The gifts that that understanding and knowledge can bring to you are important. It is not necessarily important to continue to see physically the world as you have seen it for a moment in time. It could be dizzying to you and it could lead to a car accident or such. You must keep your feet on the ground in your physical reality if you care to exist here.

A Movement Shall
Not Judge

The divinity within you is not a divinity which can be possessed. In your society you have a desire to have and to hold. Yet, in such possessiveness there is the suffering of the individual soul. The undesirable result is lack of opportunity to grow. Such relationships are oppressive. Be careful that your spiritual movement does not possess you. You must make sure that your movement does not stifle you and stunt your growth.

Your movements should accept you as you are now. The place where you are now is the place where you are meant to be. Your spiritual growth shall occur normally and naturally. There is not the need for radical change in the way one dresses, thinks, talks, and acts.

It is essential that you not use your commitment to a spiritual cause to syphon you off from other aspects of existence. You have heard the phrase "blind devotion." Individuals seeking spiritual enlightenment can be so desperate in their need for fulfillment, that they can be swayed into a particular movement and taken on a ride.

In your search for meaning and understanding, it is important that you involve yourselves in study with individuals who are non-judgmental. Many of the movements which are taking place in your society today require the tenet of judgment. Even the traditional commandments state, "Thou shall not judge." Yet, your religions and your movements seem to steadfastly judge each other. It is essential that you find a movement which makes you feel comfortable and honors you as you are. If the movement requires financial commitment, or asks you to substantially change yourself to adhere to a particular set of rules, you are probably involving yourself in a movement which seeks not to aid you, but to control you.

In the years to come, your movements shall intensify and diversify. There are going to be mass movements of a spiritual nature, as there have been mass movements of a political nature. Political movements have increased your freedom. Now is the time for spiritual movements to increase your freedom and power.

There Are No Accidents

There are no accidents. Accidents are human lessons. When an accident occurs, it is often designed to awaken the spirit that lives within. It is designed to bring life to what has been dormant. It is an opportunity for those involved to view themselves and each other in a new light.

On some level, accident is filled with design and purpose. There is always a purpose for action on this particular plane. There is always a purpose behind all chaos, pain, agony and misery.

Accidents give us the opportunity for growth and change. When people find themselves in a situation which is threatening to their life and limb, they have a new opportunity to view life with the freshness, zeal and spirit that may have been missing. Accidents are an opportunity to learn the lessons of life. They give us an opportunity to look around, and to reexamine and revalue our lives. Accidents are an opportunity to think upon those things that really matter.

Accidents give us an opportunity to come together in a way that we have not come together in the past. When we come together to offer an individual our support and love in their times of need, we are coming together in a way which makes obvious our inter-dependence upon each other. In our times of need, our enemies shall often become our greatest allies. Our enemies feel our vulnerability and it gets them in touch with their own.

It is difficult to comprehend why any aspect of one's being would create a situation which is traumatic and filled with turmoil. Yet it is in these moments of devastation that one has the opportunity to dig deep within oneself and meet the spirit within. That spirit may carry you forth into the world beyond. The same spirit that may carry you forth into the world beyond is the same spirit that may chose to keep you here. The same spirit that would give you the opportunity to move forward into the next dimension, is the same spirit that would keep you on this plane. The spirit is strength, courage, the will to live. The will to live has its roots deep within the vast, unknown area of consciousness.

Your earth plane existence has meaning, choice, and karma. The meaning is simply that you have an opportunity to learn from your experience. If your experience throws you in the middle of a tragedy and you have to fight to survive, you shall come into contact with the divine power within you that holds onto the sacredness of life. This discovery of self, this discovery of the innate and powerful wisdom within you, is awakened.

A serious accident gives you a choice. It gives you the opportunity to let go. You are given the opportunity to leave this life behind. You make a choice. The choice has meaning. You can chose to remain here. You can chose to leave. Wherever you go you will move forward in your growth. You will come in touch with your God power and experience a rebirth. A rebirth means your life takes on a new found purpose. You are reconnected with the reason you are alive. You have a new appreciation of living for the moment. The moment is a precious gift.

Q: *Is karma connected when two strangers meet and have an accident?*

A: There is not the opportunity for strangers to meet on this plane. For all those who come together, in any way, are not strangers. They always have a karmic connection.

In your thoughts you refer to a particular accident. There was a desire to kill on a different level of consciousness. The individual who died in the car accident was seeking retribution for a past wrong. In a prior existence, he and this young woman were involved in a struggle in which she was successful in having him beheaded. It is simply a way to try to balance out that particular experience. Yet, he has only succeeded in once again taking his own life. The lesson to be learned is that one cannot engage in retribution without expecting to relive and learn the lesson that retribution is not the way of the world.

The young woman involved will find herself a changed person because of this experience. She will find herself alive in a way she was not alive before the accident. The accident was a gift from the Universe.

A Not So Trivial Pursuit

You are always in pursuit. In your Constitution, you are entitled to life, liberty and the pursuit of happiness. You pursue God. At times you pursue the trivial. You are driven to accomplish, to possess, and to attain certain goals. Why is the pursuit necessary?

The pursuit is necessary because the process itself is all important. When you play your sporting activities, you say it is not whether you win or lose - it's how you play the game. The process is the all important factor in your becoming.

The "pursuit" however, suggests by the phrase, that you are seeking to attain something that you do not already possess. So the concept of pursuit is a false concept. It leads one to believe that that which is being pursued is outside of one's self. The pursuit need not be so ambitious. What you are seeking to find is already in your possession. If you continue to pursue that which is outside of yourself, the pursuit will always seem to be elusive.

There is, however, an important reason to pursue things in life which appear to be outside of yourself. In pursuing something outside of yourself, you come closer to the discovery that what you are truly looking for is within your own heart and soul. That is the educational value of the pursuit. In pursuing the outside world you discover yourself. In looking outward, you develop a way of relating to the outside world. You relate to people and their concepts. In the process of exchanging viewpoints and interrelating with others, you come a step closer to finding yourself.

Every aspect of the outside world is a part of you. Every part of you is an aspect of the outside world. So in seeking to discover the secrets of the universe external to yourself, you are really seeking to discover aspects of yourself from which you have become alienated. The bands of beauty, color and energy which make up the sun, the stars, the sky, the moon and the trees of the earth, are all elements of you. Searching externally for God is not an empty trail. God exists in all things which you observe, and in all things which you touch upon your journey. The pursuit, however, in the long run will simply reconnect you with the self from which you have become alienated. The external search beyond, shall always lead you back home.

Part Two:
Heavenly Byways

Open Your Mind

Movement or progression is the ability to get from one point to another. In your society you have developed modes of transportation. Transportation systems transport you from point A to point B. Yet you have the power to expand your consciousness so that you can become one with the universe. Then such methods of transportation are not necessary.

You will know when you have arrived. You will know when you have become one with the universe. In becoming one with the universe you shall experience an untold sense of joy, peace and equanimity. There will be no fanfare. There will simply be the sheer essence of joy. You will understand that you have found your place in existence.

What is your place in existence? Why are you where you are? Why are you creating such a difficult path? The answers to these questions are many and varied. What we seek to teach you is simply that it is not necessary for you to travel physically to gain self knowledge. It is not necessary for you to transport yourself. Your soul is divine. Your soul exists not only within your own heart but in the heart of every human that exists. You are your brother's and sister's keeper. You have often heard that phrase and wondered what it means. The essence of you is indivisible from the essence of another. We seek to teach you how to tune into the essence of others so that you can tap the knowledge and understanding they possess.

Your consciousness has the ability to travel and to "get inside" the consciousness of another. There are those of you who have experimented with Ouija boards. Often an individual energy will come on the board and will claim to be a living person. This is generally a friend or an acquaintance of the player who is working the board. What this should teach you is that the consciousness of the individual is able to move about and communicate outside of the physical body.

As you sit here today, your consciousness is active in other parts of the universe. Your consciousness is not embodied solely within your skeletal structure. Your consciousness is fluid and malleable. It can be in many different places at one time. It can exist on many different planes at the same time. Your consciousness is ever present in all parts of the universe. Your consciousness finds its present home in your physical being. That is the consciousness of which you are aware. You are aware of the consciousness which thinks, feels, hears, sees and touches. Yet there are other aspects to your consciousness. You have become alienated from them in this physical existence. You have the opportunity to become reunited with the fragmented sources of your consciousness. You shall then come to understand and know yourself better. You will then come to know and understand the universe in a more intimate way. You will have universal knowledge within your grasp.

Open your mind. Be receptive to the reunion between your soul and the fragmented sources of its consciousness. Your scientists have told you that you only use a very small portion of your brain. The remainder of your brain cells are alive and well. They are not lying dormant.

They are simply being activated in arenas in which you are not conscious. Your conscious mind protects you from this information. It believes you are not ready, willing or able to accept the complexity and the density of the information and knowledge which is truly known to your consciousness. Through these lessons you may begin several practices which should enable you to recapture your consciousness.

The first step is to begin the process of activating your brain cells. Your brain is made up of electromagnetic receptors. Components of your brain receive and send off electromagnetic materials. Your brain is like a machine, the most complex of all machines. It needs to be oiled well. It needs to be stored in a place where it will not be rained upon and rust. This simply means that you should be aware of your brain as being a part of the physical you, but also recognize its consciousness exists separate from your physical body. Your mind has the capacity to move beyond physical reality.

Begin to allow your brain the freedom it needs to communicate with the consciousness from which it has become separated. Your brain has the power to transmit information and knowledge to other parts of the universe. It has the power and the capacity to receive information and communication from various parts of the universe. It is important that you give your brain the freedom to remain as uncluttered as possible. In your daily existence this is easier said than done.

Begin the process of actualizing your brain cells by giving them permission to expand. Your brain is more elaborate than you can possibly fathom. Your limitations come from the inability of your consciousness to accept or understand the complexity of your brain. Therefore, your brain acts as a protector of itself. You have heard the

61

expression that a little knowledge is a dangerous thing. Your brain has expressed this philosophy by protecting itself with your ignorant limitations. The capacity of your mind to expand is limitless. You can save yourself from your intellectual limitations. The first step is to give your brain cells permission to expand. Affirm that it is all right for your brain to begin its proper functions. Then you can move on to the second step.

The second stage involves some practical day to day testing. Attempt to understand something of which you know nothing. You have often heard the phrase osmosis. This is learning through osmosis. This is the closest analogy that can be drawn to this particular kind of brain-mind learning.

Pick a subject you have an interest in. Discover a source of information on that particular topic. Allow your mind consciousness to leave your brain structure. Go to that place. Gather the information and knowledge. Bring it back with you to the place where you exist physically. This is no easy task. With repeated effort, you should be able to learn by allowing one aspect of your consciousness to do the work. This could be remarkably productive. You can be in more than one place at the same time. You can have one aspect of your consciousness working on a project for you on one level, while another aspect of your consciousness works elsewhere.

This process is already being used by your brain-mind structure. You are simply not aware of it. You are not conscious of the ways in which your energies pick up and deliver information. You receive information in what you call your unconscious. Yet in reality there is no such thing as an unconscious. There is only another conscious aspect of yourself of which you are presently not aware.

This information gathering technique is being used by

your government at the present time. Your government employees literally hundreds of psychic individuals. They work for the government attempting to learn secrets from the Soviet Union. They seek to keep this information from you. It is possible to use this method of information collection in ways which are not for the good of all. We trust that those who read this information, and partake of its use and benefit, will use it.

You may, in the weeks to come, find yourselves being able to converse with your loved ones without use of the telephone. You can develop telepathic conversational ability simply by practicing. Arrange with your friends for a particular time of day to attempt this kind of communication. At an assigned time, sit down and begin a meditation. Open up your brain-mind structure to allow reception of information from your friends. You can send back a response with your brain-mind consciousness.

This method is similar to what has traditionally been known as prayer. Prayers are often perceived as one-sided. There are very few who claim to have heard back from God. In these communications, the information should not be one-sided. Give and you shall receive. Following your prayers, open your mind to receive.

Q: *Why should we encourage people to see beyond physical reality when they've chosen to be in physical existence for this life?*

A: Not all people should be encouraged to see beyond physical reality. There may be those who see beyond it and would use such powers in "negative" ways. People who are desirous of expanding their consciousness and self-awareness will seek out this information. They will find it. It will be fruitful for them in their method of self-growth. The value in becoming aware

SOJOURNS OF THE SOUL

of one's brain power is simply that it gets you back in touch with your ultimate divinity and your capacity to become one with the universe. It is assumed that one's goal in life is to ultimately arrive at a state where there does not exist a separation between oneself and the universe at large. Recognition of one's presence in the form of consciousness all over the universe is a step towards experiencing this reality.

The Human Transformer

In your daily life you have many opportunities to observe a transformational process. A rice kernel is hard and small. By placing it in boiling water, you can watch it grow, expand, change dimensions. It becomes soft, full, and capable of providing nourishment. Learn from observing these transformational processes. You too can create such transformations in your own life.

The first step is to recognize what you would like to transform. Recognition is a big step. In recognition, there is awareness. In awareness there is the opportunity to transform. So be aware, be alert. Be awake with all of your senses, including your psychic sense. What do you want to change?

Transformation can appear in front of your very eyes, or it can take a period of time. Ultimately the length of time that it takes is up to you. There are times when changes should be gradual and there are times when changes should be swift.

Once you have recognized what needs to be transformed, you then need to decide upon the ultimate "product" you wish to create. Imagine the "product" with all of your senses. In the vision you give power to the process. See it, hear it, feel it, smell it. Begin the process of creating it with your imagination. Your imagination is one of your greatest guides. Follow your imagination.

Now you have recognized what you would like to

transform. You have imagined what you would like to create. You must then address the steps in between the recognition and the ultimate creation.

Between point "a"—the recognition, and point "b"—the ultimate creation, there are stepping stones which create a path for you to travel. On the first stepping stone, you must trigger the aspect of your mental processes that can activate other realities. This means you need to establish the connection between the consciousness within you and the consciousness outside of you. This may need some explanation.

Some of you perceive that the entire possessory body of your soul is within your physical being. When you go through a process such as astral-projection, you perceive that you leave your body and you travel to another place. In actuality, what occurs is that you simply become aware of your consciousness as it exists in other places. Your consciousness exists everywhere at this very moment. You need to trigger your ability to become aware of your consciousness as it exists in other places. You need to establish a communication between the consciousness which is within your physical body and the consciousness which is outside of your physical body.

The first stepping stone is to trigger an aspect of your consciousness which is "separate" from your physical body. This step may take time to develop. You need to practice a belief system which holds that your consciousness is ever present, and exists with a sense of constancy all over the universe. Then you can tap into the aspects of your consciousness which exist in other places.

By tapping into other aspects of your consciousness, you can tap into more of your power. This can be very fruitful for you. The consciousness which exists outside of the physical plane is not limited by your brain-mind function. Your brain capacity can be your greatest friend or your most limiting enemy. You have the opportunity to develop a connection with your consciousness as it exists outside of your physical body. When you do this, you activate the cellular-like structure which makes up your consciousness. In developing a connection with and stimulating that structure, you can communicate with various aspects of yourself in other places. You can draw upon the information that is contained within the cellular structure.

You need to decide how you want to transform a particular situation. You need to use your mind's consciousness to create steps which are intellectual and/or emotional in nature. Generally for a transformation to occur, there has to be a change in the emotional, as well as the intellectual being. Fathom for a moment the process you will use in order to achieve your ultimate end. When you design that process for yourself, you can then activate the consciousness which is separate from your physical self, and use the power from that form of consciousness to begin the wheels turning on this process of transformation. As the wheels begin to turn, you shall find that the concept, idea or physical property that you seek to transform will become malleable in its nature.

You may perceive time as a past, present, and future. You may perceive time to be linear. When you leave this physical plane, you learn that time is not linear. Time is ever present. You may perceive that you have a past, present and future life. In reality, you are living all of your lives at the same time. Your concept of linear time is an illusion. Recognize that at this very time you are living lives in different dimensions of reality. The lives you are living in those different dimensions have particular characteristics and attributes which may be useful for you in this particular life.

Seek to connect with the soul aspect of yourself which is in existence in another body in another dimension of reality. If you seek to acquire "patience," you can check into yourself as you exist in a Job-like character. You can draw upon the patience that you have in that particular life and incorporate it into your being. You have within you the power to create all of the characteristics which you would like to have. You also have the power to create all of the other things you seek to enjoy out of life—a good relationship, material possessions, and spiritual enlightenment.

Q: *I understand what you are saying on an intellectual level about uniting with the consciousness outside of myself. But if I'm to go home, and I want to do this on a mechanical basis, I think I'd be lost. How can I begin?*

A: To begin, envision all of the qualities that you would like to have, or all of the things that you would like to draw to you in your life. Then envision the presence of those particular characteristics or properties in another part of your being. Get an image of this in your mind. You then recognize and give power to the existence of the quality outside of your present sense of self.

Then imagine a golden cord which ties your consciousness to the external consciousness you are attempting to tap. Through the gold cord you will receive the energy, information, quality and so forth. Imagine yourself as you exist in another life. If you are seeking to find virtue, imagine yourself as a monk. Imagine the cord connecting your consciousness with that of the monk and drawing the virtue towards you. Envision the virtue integrating with your consciousness and becoming a part of your being.

Q: *Assuming that a collective consciousness has power, if I want to transform a situation, how much does other people's energy effect what I would like to design for myself?*

A: You have the ultimate control and power to create your own destiny. There may be others who seek to sabotage you. The interaction that takes place between these different energy forms is crucial for your own growth. On one level of your being, you are drawing the adversity to you. It is only through such adversity that you may have the opportunity to strengthen your position or to change it if the need be. All the adversity that you draw has really been drawn to you by some aspect of yourself. The aspect needed to be tested. Although you may perceive the adversity to be coming from places outside of yourself to block your growth, a magnetic quality of your own is bringing it to you.

You can help change the course of the world for others if they allow you to do it. You see this in healing work. You may be working with an individual who is tremendously ill. No matter what your powers could do in terms of healing this individual, the sick person ultimately has the power to accept or reject the healing energy. You cannot change the course of events for those who do not desire to have them changed.

Astral-Projection: A Lesson From the Star Esoterica

W e now venture forth into the land of wonderment known as the "sky." The skies have as their blessed inhabitants the sparkling entities which you call stars. We begin with a voyage to the Star Esoterica. This star is in your heaven far away—so far away that you are unaware of it. It is so far away that your scientists have not yet discovered it. This particular star was at one point a portion of your consciousness. This star gave you the breath of life.

"Esoterica" means "something a little bit unusual." There is something most unusual about this star. Esoterica hosts a group of beings who desire to come to your plane to give you the gift of Love and Joy. They wish to plade a lei upon your body. It is not a way to bind you. It is a way to give you eternal life. It is the gift of eternal Spring.

A being named Rafini will be coming to speak with you. He is an embodiment of a multitudinous form of consciousness. He aims to teach you that your consciousness is linked up to other forms of consciousness in the Universe. The consciousness which you possess as your own belongs to the Universe. The stream of consciousness which flows through you exists in many places. It connects each of you. We desire to make these connections more solid.

This planet is a blessed home to each of you. This planet is also blessed home to each of us. Yet this planet is in need of healing. Open your hearts and your souls. Be more receptive. We come to you at this time to help you set yourselves free.

RAFINI:

There is a star in the sky known as Esoterica. Esoterica is in a galaxy beyond your Milky Way. Esoterica is in a star system which has not yet been discovered by your scientists.

Esoterica may be visited through the art of Soul Travel. I intend to give you some simple steps to aid you in your ability to travel through the universe. Share the information you obtain with those around you.

Astral-projection has been looked upon as a dream state. Dream state it is not! Awakened, you have the ability to go beyond the limits of your physical reality.

Here are some simple steps:

ONE: *The ability you have to become aware of your consciousness as separate from your body is innate. It is easier for you to experience this separation when you find yourself in a state of exhaustion, depression, sickness, or in any state when you are feeling the heaviness and sedation of your body. The heaviness of your body will hold you down. This will allow the feeling of separation to occur.*

Allow yourself the opportunity to be set free! Give yourself permission to be free. Give yourself the assurance that you will return and everything will be normal. The biggest inhibiting factor to the release of your consciousness is fear. Fear holds you back.

Acknowledge that the universe is a safe, warm and beauti-

ful place. The universe is ready and willing to accept you as a traveler. The universe is not like it is portrayed in your movies. There are no bad guys waiting to shoot you.

You are welcome here. It will be a delight for those of us on the other planes to experience you as a visitor. There are no boundaries. It is not necessary to obtain a passport, nor is it necessary for you to get your shots. You simply have to allow yourself the opportunity to separate.

If you are working hard, feeling stress, and looking for an easy way to replenish what seems to be lost by your daily activities, visit the untold universe by Astral-projection.

TWO: *It is essential, that you practice. You can practice in small ways, or you can practice in big ways. I suggest you start small.*

When you are awake, lying in your bed, give yourself permission to rise above your body momentarily. Be aware of your consciousness as it exists outside of your particular head space. Allow yourself the opportunity to go a short distance.

If you continue with your meditations, your consciousness will begin this process on its own. If you are involved in activities which allow for introspection, continue with those activities. You should be fortunate enough to begin the process of separation without even trying. If you try too hard, you may prevent this shift in awareness from occuring.

If you have gotten to the point where you are able to shift the awareness of your consciousness in a small way, then proceed to the next step. The next step is to allow yourself permission to visit your friends in the universe beyond.

THREE: *Each of you have guides who are willing to help you, and to be your travelmates. It is essential for you to awaken yourselves to these individual guides. Wake up to their desire to guide you. Your guides are waving to you as you*

73

drive down the street. Your guides are looking at you when you look at yourself in a mirror. They are wanting to be heard, wanting to be seen, and wanting to be touched. Awaken your hearts and your souls to those around you. In your moments of silent meditation give them permission to come into your life. Allow them to be your companions. Allow for them to love you. They are seeking to take you by the hand and dance the dance of light. They are seeking to join you on the journey back home.

Sometimes it is difficult for human beings to allow other human beings to love them. Perhaps it is easier to allow yourself to be loved by those you cannot see. You do not have the same vulnerability with us. You do not have the same insecurities and fears with us. We give you the promise of the future. We give you the promise that we shall always be here. We shall never leave your side. We are connected by the forever of time.

Envision a cord which connects you with Esoterica. This beam of light shall give you power. It will connect you with our consciousness and provide you with an umbilical cord home.

The Third Eye
Star Connection: Altair

Altair is a star which shines brightly in your sky. It cannot be seen by the naked eye. It can be viewed your spiritual eye, the third eye.

Each of you has the ability to perceive what is beyond your current physical vision. The tool which you have been given to enable you to see that which cannot be seen, is the third eye. The third eye is located in the middle of your forebrain. It is a great psychic sack of power. It gives you the ability to make connections.

The star Altair is inhabited by a group of entities with many different faces. These individuals are seeking to connect with you. The connection can be made with your third eye.

Altair was the beginning for many of you. Altair can act as a spaceship and reconnect you with the original source. The star of Altair is waiting at this time to board all of its passengers to take the trip home.

To activate your third eye each of you should begin a very silent and holy meditation. Sit by yourself, or with others who are seeking to accomplish the same goals. Experience a moment of silence. In this moment of silence begin to feel a tremendous amount of pressure and sensitivity in the area between your two natural eyes on your forehead. It will feel as though you are about to experience a headache.

When you feel this particular pain, release it. Pain is simply a yearning to let go of something. When you feel this pain in your conscious mind, seek to let it be free. Let the pain go outward, upward, and beyond your sphere of reality. When the pain is gone, there should be an opening. In the opening a divine presence shall seek to connect you with the beings from Altair.

Communication will generally come in the form of a stream of consciousness. Make way for thought to enter your mind. Make way for sights to enter your vision. Make way for sounds to enter your realm of hearing. The sights and sounds of this new consciousness will seek to envelop and fulfill you.

The connection once established shall always be established. The connection once experienced shall always be experienced. The connection once known shall always be known.

It is important that you continue to take time out of your lives to meditate, to release your pain, and to establish communion with those entities who seek to love, guide, and teach you. They will help you to understand that the ups and downs are really a smaller part of the greater whole. It is the greater whole with which they seek to connect you.

Your guides can give you companionship, courage, strength and guidance. They are friends not unlike those who surround you in your physical existence. However, they will always be there. It is constancy, faith and loyalty that you shall experience in this relationship.

Your spiritual companions give you the holiest of all loves. They love you unconditionally. You cannot betray them. You cannot hurt or scar them. They love you unconditionally no matter what you do. Experience unconditional love in its fullness.

Altair is a beautiful place. Altair is a real place. Altair is a place which seeks to be your home. When you are sleeping, when you are dreaming, when you are desiring a new vacation spot, think of Altair. Transportation to Altair is very inexpensive. Survival in Altair costs little.

Q: *Altair seems to represent the Trinity. There are the symbols of freedom, power, and unconditional love. Is it Altair that other religions have been focused on when they refer to a trinity?*

A: The trinity of which you speak is ever-present in Altair. Symbolism is extremely important. However, we seek to get beyond symbolism. Traditional religions have been immersed in symbolism. We hope to get beyond the symbolism, and help you experience the true essence of the teachings. Symbolically we may be perceived of as being the Trinity. However, we choose to get beyond the symbolism.

Aspects of the World Beyond

You contemplate the world beyond in some of your wildest moments. It is important that you not spend too much time looking forward to the world beyond. It is beyond you at this moment for a reason. It is essential for you to enjoy the present. Be here now. Do not devote tremendous numbers of hours trying to comprehend the next life. The life which you are living now is the life which is most important. With that word of caution we shall discuss the world beyond.

There are many different experiences awaiting you beyond your physical plane. When you transform your physical life you may head to a variety of different dimensions. There is not one absolute place where all beings go when they pass this plane. Life beyond your physical world is a many-splendored experience indeed.

You alone will have the decision as to where you will go when it is your time to move on. The decision will not be made by some God outside of yourself. You may be advised and guided. You may seek to learn from others so that you may place yourself in the dimension which will hold the most learning for you. The decision will remain yours. There are many different options.

The first option, one that you are the most familiar with, is a reincarnational experience back upon the earth plane. The earth plane has been created by you for several reasons. First of all, physical expression offers many learning opportunities. It gives you an understanding of limitation. Understanding limit is necessary before you can move beyond and experience the unlimited. Your physical world limits you, but it also enhances your growth towards unlimited consciousness.

Secondly, your physical world allows you to begin to integrate your different aspects. You are given the opportunity to intertwine the mind, body and spirit.

Your physical world gives you an opportunity to understand your present separateness from the God force. In understanding your separation, you can come closer to a union with God. Recognize that God is within you. God is within every aspect of your being. You are a co-creator with God. You must come into alignment with the God force. Your physical existence allows you to begin to understand the inherent connection between your own soul and the soul of all consciousness.

When you determine that it is time for you to leave the physical plane, and to dance for a while in another sphere, you have various options awaiting you. You can spend time hovering about in what is known to you as the ethereal plane. The ethereal plane and the astral plane are intimately connected. In many places it is hard to distinguish between the two.

The ethereal plane is the plane of consciousness which acts as a protectorate of your physical world. On this particular plane, you will have the opportunity to experience reunion with the loved ones from whom you have momentarily been separated. You have the opportunity to integrate yourself, and to mingle with physical consciousness; however, you will not be in a physical state. In this mingling, you can begin to understand the power of cohesion. You can see yourself as being a part of the physical world, although you are no longer embodied. Here you have the opportunity to compre-hend the connection between physical and non-physical consciousness. The ethereal plane is a place where you would not likely want to spend a tremendous amount of time. The understanding that you glean from being there will enhance what you have to learn on the astral plane.

As you move beyond the ethereal plane, you enter the astral plane. The astral plane is really a grand playground. In this place you can manifest all that you have ever desired. You know that thought is energy. On this plane every thought that you think becomes reality. You have the power to create all that you have ever desired. On this plane one must have developed an understanding of the good will force of the universe. You can imagine how it would be if the consciousness here was still grappling with the physical issues of power, competition, jealousy and revenge.

On the astral plane we are developing a "collective consciousness" on a scale which may be beyond your imagination. We are coming together into a force which represents a multitude of different beings. In your society individuals have differences in their personalities and physical appearances. You have separations of race, sex, age and so forth. In this particular reality there are no such separations. This does not mean that there are not individual essences, and an ability to distinguish one energy from another. However, the essences which dis-tinguish us here are pure. Every essence has a distinct vibration. It is not a vibration which can be judged the way you in your society tend to judge the differences between individuals. When these different vibrational energies come together there is a tremendous ability to create a wondrous experience for one and all.

Why even bother to combine consciousness when each

individual consciousness has the ability to create one's own reality? On this plane one loses the desire to distinguish between individual consciousness. On this plane there is an understanding that we are all one and the same. There is a recognition that the beautiful, loving, divine God-like energy from which we were birthed, is the energy with which we seek to reunite. In coming together in union with each other there is a sense of accomplishment. There is a sense of coming home. This is a reunion that has been looked forward to since the beginning of time.

In your traditional religions you are taught about heaven. However, in order to gain entry into heaven, you have been obliged to follow a set of rules. The heaven we invite you to experience is not a heaven where judgment exists. This heaven is a place for all beings who have learned about the God within them and long to set the God free.

As we continue upon our lessons, we shall discuss various steps that one can take to allow this God to be free. These steps are advisory steps. They need not necessarily be taken. There is no judgment that the steps laid out by other leaders within your society are improper steps. Each individual has his or her own path to enlightenment. Every step that an individual takes is a step in the right direction.

Q: *You said the astral plane is a playground where we have the power to create things for ourselves. Don't we have that ability now, on the earth plane, if we would only cultivate it?*

A: Certainly you have that ability now. You simply don't believe it through and through. In order for you to practice the art of manifesting successfully, you must convince all aspects of yourself to believe this power exists. Your intellect may believe it but your emotional being may not. There may be some aspects of your being which maintain their skepticism. As long as you maintain this doubt, you may not be able to put this power into practice successfully.

Q: *Do you exist on the astral plane and then return to earth through channeling, as a form of energy?*

A: I never really leave the astral plane, or any other plane on which my consciousness exists. We have the ability to be in many places at one time. I don't ever really leave. I am simply permitting various aspects of my consciousness to depart for a moment. The essence of my being maintains itself here as well as in all of the other places where I work. This particular moment is not the only moment in which I exist. I exist in many places at the "same time."

Three Steps
To Enlightenment

Enlightenment has been defined in many ways. It has been thought of as entry into heaven. It has been defined as God consciousness. We speak of enlightenment as a state where one can transcend the physical world and exist on a plane where thoughts are manifested into reality. On the astral plane your thoughts manifest into reality with immediacy.

The astral plane is not by any means the end all. The astral plane is merely a stepping stone. In the astral plane there still exists the separation between one's own spiritual consciousness and the consciousness of the rest of existence. It is a step beyond the astral plane where one must go in order to experience true union with the universal life flow of energy. Here are a few steps that you may engage in, in order to ease your own entry into the astral plane. The astral plane exists for your learning, your knowledge, and your pleasure. It exists as a playground where you can come to know yourself better. You will become more intimate with energies which you now perceive to be external to yourself.

The astral plane invites each of you to come. Life here is abundant and full. The concepts of scarcity and limitation do not exist.

STEP NUMBER ONE:

Practice metaphysical thinking. Believe in your power to create your own reality. Place your heart and soul into believing in this power. Your heart and soul are the directors of your consciousness.

You must understand the true essence of which you are made. The true essence you are made of is spiritual and divine. You must actively incorporate this divinity into your daily existence. Do this by affirming what you believe.

Affirming is stating what you believe to be true in a positive and loving way. Do not meditate upon accomplishing such desires in the future. Think on them as though they exist now. Experience your affirmations in the present. You must place emphasis and power in the present.

The present time is all you have. The present is the past, the future and this very moment rolled into one. The present is infinite. The present is timeless. Give respect to the period of now. Revere your experience of the moment. Do not continue to focus upon your yesteryears or your tomorrows. Do not focus your energy upon trying to accomplish a gain in the future. It is this very moment in which you are alive. Focus on this present moment. Focus on the life and breath you are giving to the universe in this second. You were not put on this plane to live for tomorrow. You were put here to live for today.

STEP NUMBER TWO:

Practice unconditional love. Among your enemies are your brothers and sisters. Your closest allies are among those whom you despise. All beings on this planet are made from the divine essence of God. Within each of these individuals, God live. Do not worship this force as an external force. This force lives within you. This is the force that gives you your heartbeat and your lung capacity. It is a gift you give yourself.

Unconditional love is easy to express in words. It is difficult to express in action. It is essential that you begin the process of loving unconditionally. Express this love in action.

Here is a homework assignment for you. Every day, take an opportunity to express unconditional love. Take the opportunity to love your enemy as yourself. Find the God force in someone you find to be undesirable. In recognizing the God force within all things, you will begin to re-establish the inter-connectedness of all aspects of life.

STEP NUMBER THREE:

Respect nature. Nature is your greatest friend. You have abused nature and treated it as though it were an enemy. It has fought back in self-defense. When you experience cataclysmic events such as earthquakes and volcanoes, you are hearing nature talk. Nature is trying to tell you that you are sharing the same planet.

It is essential that you begin to view the animal and plant kingdoms as your brothers and sisters. The animal and plant kingdoms are very much alive. Revere the members of your animal and plant communities. You have a great deal to learn from the way nature and animals are able to exist with each other harmoniously.

The world in which you exist is a sacred place. It was created by each of you for your own growth. Why, then, do you torment the earth so? Why, then, do you torment each other so? All existence is here to teach, love and guide you. Treasure it. If you abuse your earth, you are abusing yourself. If you abuse any aspect of creative existence, you are setting yourself back. If you begin to practice these three simple steps, you should find yourself evolving spiritually at a very rapid rate.

Q: *You said we should focus our energy on the present. What role do memories and fantasies have in our lives?*

A: Memories and fantasies are very much alive. Memories and fantasies do not really represent a period of time other than the present. You may remember something as a past experience. Yet it is alive in the present if it is a thought in your mind. It is this alive quality that you must cherish. The role it is playing in your present is important. The reason it remains alive for you in your mind is significant. Try to understand why it remains alive and integrate the meaning into your present.

Your fantasies also represent the present. Your fantasies may be dreams or hopes for another time. Yet the fact that they are alive now in your mind gives them power in your present. The imagery in affirmations can be termed fantasy. Affirmations are a way of applying present power to a particular fantasy. This is a way of making the future alive in the moment. Give fantasies power in the present. Through this process, the reality of the fantasy shall come true for you in another moment of your present.

*Three Steps
to the Impossible*

A challenge should greet you every morning when you take your first breath. A challenge should never be absent from your life. Challenges inspire you to go forward in your moments of fatigue and defeat.

There are many ways to challenge yourself. It is the ultimate challenge that we shall discuss. The challenge of the soul. The soul for many of you remains dormant. Your souls are asleep. Awaken from your slumber. Allow your soul to expand, grow and develop. This is the soul's challenge.

A challenge is doing something which has not been done before. Dare to go beyond your wildest dreams. Travel in a steady, uphill way. You will challenge yourselves in many ways in the times to come. Here are three steps to meeting the impossible challenge.

STEP NUMBER ONE: What you have defined as "impossible," is only what you are unable to perceive and justify intellectually. In many ways your intellect prohibits you from seeking the ultimate challenge. This challenge is awaiting you every moment. Seek to achieve what you believe to be impossible. Choose a challenge which if achieved, would bring you some benefit.

In other words, you may choose to see a table rise in front of you. This act may have benefit in that it will teach you that you can achieve what you think is impossible. Yet the accomplishment of the table rising will not give you any particular benefit in life. Therefore choose an achievement that will be of great benefit to you or someone you love.

STEP NUMBER TWO: Once you have achieved what you previously thought to be impossible, you are ready for the next step. Step Number One may take longer than you think. Perhaps a year or two. Step Number One involves tremendous commitment. But once you have achieved the impossible, you are ready to proceed to Step Number Two.

Step Number Two involves teaching impossibilities. You will be challenged immensely by teaching impossibilities to others. You should not endeavor to teach those who do not wish to learn. You should not endeavor to preach to those who have deaf ears. Choose to share your knowledge and power with those who are interested.

Develop an intellectual framework into which you can put your philosophy. You do exist on the physical plane. The physical plane involves dealing with the intellect. Your intellects may be barriers at times, but they can also serve you well. They can frame your ideas such that you can then articulate them to others.

It is important that you begin the process of communication with those around you. You must communicate directly and clearly. When you have taught another individual that they can achieve the impossible, and they have actually achieved the impossible, you are ready to move on to Step Number Three.

STEP NUMBER THREE: Step number three involves the use of your powers to benefit the entire universe.

Your consciousness has the power to travel and to

work in worlds which have yet to be unfolded. Begin the process of using your consciousness as a teacher when you are not within your physical body. Allow your consciousness the freedom and opportunity to travel in your moments of slumber. You can be teachers of light in the universe. The universe welcomes you. The universe needs you. The universe looks forward to your teaching companionship.

Q: *How do you "let go," once you've achieved a goal? How do you move on?*

A: If it's time to let go, you will let go. If there is a "holding on"—it generally means the time has not come for release. There are times when it is important to hold tight. You cannot release before your learning has sunk in.

If you are ready to release, it is very simple to do. Allow your conscious mind the opportunity to let go. Imagine, if you will, that what you desire to be released is inside of a balloon, floating upward and onward into the sky. Everything you wish to send off into the universe should be blessed, and sent off with love. Do not push out what is not ready to go. Once it is ready, you can simply give it an "airlift."

Q: *What is impossible in physical reality? Surely you can't jump off a building at 30,000 feet and survive?*

A: I don't believe there is anything that is impossible in physical reality. It's just that everybody believes that if you jump off this building you will die. And if you believe that, you shall die. Of course, there have been many examples in your history of the "impossible" occurring. Most people believe that if you are nailed to a cross you would die. Do you understand?

The Magic of Numbers

Numerology is the study of numbers and how those numbers relate to varying aspects of your life. You study numbers in your arithmetic classes. Yet the meaning of numbers escapes you. Numbers are not only symbols. Numbers carry a tremendous amount of energy within their graphic form. As you make a graphic form, you are creating an energy sensation. Begin to pay attention to the numbers in your life. Pay attention to the details in your life. Pay attention to the ways in which numbers relate to your wants, your needs, your desires, your future aspirations, and your hopes for tomorrow.

You are encouraged to begin the study of numerology. Begin to look upon numbers as a puzzle. Numerology is the cosmic connection of the energy form of numbers to the universal flow of being. In your life there are many numbers that you need to begin to pay attention to. The first is your date of birth. Your birthdate is not just a mere number form. It is an astrological connotation of how your life is perceived to be.

Your birthdate contains several important numbers. The first number is the day of the month you were born. Pay very close attention to this day. The second number which has tremendous power is the number of the month of the year that you were born. Beginning with January as month number one, count down and find the number of the month in which you were born. Then take recognition of the year in which you were born. The year is most important. You then have the day, the month and the year.

All of these numbers fit together in a most meaningful way. They are not simply a way of recording your entry onto the earth plane. Through these numbers you can learn a tremendous amount about yourself, about your life, about your expectations, and about the obstacles in your existence.

Take the date on which you were born, then the month and then the year. Add them together. You will come up with the grand total. The grand total of these numbers is a significant number for you. It is the number of your cosmic energy form.

Begin to understand that those numbers are magic numbers in your life. I speak now of the total of these numbers. They are your lucky numbers.

Whenever you have a choice about where you are going to stand in line, or where you are going to sit in the theatre, or where you are going to spend your money, you are encouraged to think about these numbers. Place yourself in a line that has these numbers. Follow their course.

Accept these numbers as a gift. The gift was given to each of you at birth. The numbers are a gift of love, a gift of strength, a gift of guidance.

The lesson today is very simple. Pay attention to the simplicity of the lessons. Mere simplicity does not mean there is not depth of meaning. The lessons are meant to be simple so that you can understand them and remember them as time goes by.

Q: *I have known for a long time that numbers have power in my life. Yet I have math anxiety. What does it mean to suffer from math anxiety?*

A: There are many who suffer from this complex. It is more prevalent among women than men. As we have mentioned, you live in a physical, left-brain, male oriented world. Math anxiety is simply setting your-self up so that you cannot operate in a man's world. One of the most certain ways of rejecting the male world is to reject math. Math and men go hand in hand. Men are always trying to mathematically prove and disprove things. Your rejection of math has a lot to do with the rejection of the left-brain world.

I'm not encouraging you to learn how to do long division. I'm just asking you to pay attention to the birth numbers in your life. There is no anxiety to it. Your birth date is surrounded with lots of love.

The Art of Healing
With Love

The art of healing is an ancient art. It has its origins in the beginning of consciousness. The essence of every human being contains healing power.

All illness is brought upon you by some aspect of your being. Therefore, all illness can be taken away by that same aspect of your being. This is a very simple concept. Yet it is ignored by your scientists and your medical doctors.

To begin the process of self healing, you must begin the process of self-loving. All healing energy comes from love. Love is the divine essence of all things. Love is beyond emotion. Love is the God force of the universe. Love propels all healing power into existence.

Healing energy can come to you in many ways. It comes through prayer, through meditation, and through creative visualization. Visualize the healing you would like to see take place. Create the reality with your thought patterns and energy fields.

Your hands contain perhaps the most vital source of healing energy that exists. By merely placing your hand upon the part of an individual which is in pain, you shall be giving them nature's best healing energy.

Young mothers often give their children a kiss when then hurt. You may think the kiss only made the child believe the pain got better. However, the kiss itself transmitted loving energy to the source of pain. In that transmission, the pain is alleviated.

The child also believed that she was going to get better. The mind of the person who has taken ill is in the front seat driving. What that mind expects to happen is essential in determining the outcome of any illness.

Nature is the finest of all healers. The cycles of nature provide spiritual regeneration. The earth contains natural remedies that can be used to cure the woes of the world.

In your culture there is a tremendous emphasis on the use of drugs for healing and for curing disease. This emphasis does not take into account that disease is created by the mind in the first place. There may well be an organic cause to a particular illness. Yet the organic cause would not exist within the individual unless the individual gave permission on some level of her being for this disfunction to exist. Before drugs are used, the individual's mind and spirit must be considered. The mind and the spirit are the directors of the disease. The mind and the spirit will determine whether or not the drugs used will be effective.

This is not to say that there is not a place for your medical sciences. Your medical sciences have achieved miraculous recoveries. There needs to be recognition that the miraculous recovery occurred, not solely because medical science was able to support physical life for a little longer, but because the individual's mind and spirit gave permission for that recovery to occur.

Illness is a way that many individuals in your society have devised to come to terms with relevant issues in their lives. When a person becomes seriously ill, all life for that individual changes. The entire focus and direction of life is altered. An individual who finds himself in a life threatening situation is being given options. He must choose life or he must choose death. He must determine whether or not his wealth would be better pursued on this particular plane or on another. Life's greatest meaning comes when one is faced with the prospect of death.

Close Your Eyes for Increased Vision: A White Light Meditation

Magic is simply what your intellect does not allow you to perceive. Magic is the creation of fantasy and illusion from facts and reality. Illusion and reality are really one and the same. All life is a matter of perception.

Perception is the vision you allow yourself to have. You do not allow yourself to see in a multi-dimensional way. You do not allow yourself to see what you can observe from an angle which is 380 degrees. You do not give yourself this freedom. If you do not give yourself this freedom, the freedom shall not be yours.

You can train yourself to perceive in a multi-dimensional way. The world is more meaningful when you can view it from a perspective of 380 degrees.

One way for you to gain this perspective is to begin to practice the art of astral travel. This art has been discussed elsewhere in these pages. If you travel in this way, your vision will not be limited to what your eyes can see. Your vision will become awakened to what your consciousness can observe.

Your consciousness is really the eye through which you observe the universe. Your eyes limit you. You are unable to perceive other worlds through your eyes. Developing your consciousness is developing your sight.

When you develop your consciousness, you develop the ability to perceive. Begin working on the art of perception. Develop your awareness. Simply be aware of those things which are in your presence. To gain such awareness, it is helpful to begin the practice of meditation.

In meditation you close your eyes. Closing your eyes is a beginning step towards developing greater vision. Closing your eyes awakens the awareness of your other senses. When you close your eyes you are shutting off the stimulus which exists in the outside world. When you turn off the static, you begin to truly perceive.

Meditation is simple. Here is a meditation you can do every day:

1) Sit yourself down. Sit in a quiet place. Take the phone off the hook. The children should be in a place where they cannot disturb you. Your pets should be outside. Close the door of the world behind you.

2) Sit or lie in a relaxed position in a comfortable place. Wear comfortable clothing. Close your eyes.

3) Relax and breathe deeply. Sense the air that you breathe. It is not simply air. It is energy of the cosmos. Allow this energy to fill your lungs to their deepest capacity. Then breathe out. As you breathe the air out, become aware that you are creating an energy exchange. You are exchanging energy with the universe. The universe is filling you up, and as you breathe out, you are re-filling the universe with that same creative force.

The energy you breathe in and out is not just a part of the universe. It is also a part of you. Continue breathing, slowly and surely. Recognize that you are becoming more closely aligned with universal energy. As you breathe in the air, envision the air as sparkling white light.

4) Move this white light energy into your brain. Move it to the left side and swirl it around. Then move the light into the right side of the brain. Swirl it around the right side of the brain. Then move the light down behind your head into the back of your neck.

Work the light into the neck area. Then move down through the neck into the shoulders. Move the light into your shoulder muscles. Relax them.

Then move the light into your lungs. First your left lung. Then your right lung. Cleanse them with deep white light breaths.

Then move the light into your lower body. Move it into your heart area. Unfold all the loving, emotional aspects of yourself. Then move the light into the chest area of your body.

Expand the light so that it fills your arms and your hands. Move it into each finger. Move it into the lower part of your abdomen and into your liver, kidneys and your spleen. Continue to expand the light. Then move the light down into the left leg. Then move it into the right leg. Fill your legs with this beautiful, positive, loving energy. Have the white light enter your feet. Fill each of your toes.

5) Expand the light to envelope your entire being. Become aware that you are all things. Understand that the energy which is filling your body is the same energy that gave you birth. This energy is God. Allow yourself to experience this marvelous form of creation.

6) See this white light expanding outward from your body to fill the room in which you sit. Expanding it further to fill the entire home in which you reside. Then move the white light outward to fill your neighborhood and then your city. After the white light has filled your entire city, expand it to fill your entire state. Then expand it to fill your entire country. Then move it outward to envelop the oceans and the other countries of your earth. After the white light has completely enveloped the earth with its love, project the light outward into the universes beyond your plane.

7) While all creation is ensconced in this energy, you may repeat your daily affirmations. Affirmations are the desires you wish to manifest. They are the goals you have for yourself and for the world around you. Put your thoughts into action. Take your dreams and mentally project them.

8) After your affirmations are completed, begin to move the light, step by step, back into the forebrain area of your head. Come to open your eyes slowly. This completes your meditation.

Meditation is a way to communicate with God. Through meditation you shall come to know God. The God is you.

Part Three:
Terra Lane

Love and Lust

In your physical world you experience lust as a desire of the body. Yet when you feel lustful desire, whether it be sexual or otherwise, you are receiving a signal from the soul.

When one feels lust, what one is truly longing for is the connection with another soul. This desire for connection is diverted into a sexual craving. This occurs because your society is focused on the physical body.

When you are focused in the physical, and you long for a connection, the desire is translated into a physical longing for another human body. You desire to experience closeness. You desire to be fulfilled. You long for love. When you are experiencing the desire to communicate with another solely on a sexual level, what you are truly longing for is the ability to connect with an individual on a very spiritual level. The physical body interprets spiritual longing as physical desire.

Many of you experience periods when you feel powerful lustful desire. Do not fear these feelings. Instead, channel this energy into love. Love can be the end result of a lustful feeling. Lust can grow into love. Lustful energies can be channeled into a higher force.

When you act upon your lustful desires, you open yourself. You open your body. You open your spirit. You open your immune system. If you allow yourself to act on your feelings of lust at all times, you may welcome feelings of fear and self- loathing. These feelings may invite disease to inhabit your being. Acting in love serves to protect you.

This is not to say that you are morally prohibited from having your sexual needs met. It is important, however, to attend to your own needs, whatever they may be, in a way which encourages self-love. If you are able to freely love others around you in the physical sense, and remain proud, beautiful, and secure within yourself, all the more power to you. However, if you experience fear, doubt and self-hatred when you engage in this kind of sexual conduct, you are opening yourself up to experience disease.

When you are able to consciously determine whether to experience lust in a "negative" or "positive" way, you have reached a turning point in your life. Take those lustful feelings and turn them into a loving energy exchange. Experience love coming back to you in the same way that you are sending it out. There is nothing more beautiful than the exchange of love. There is nothing more sacred than true communion. "Making love" is an ultimate form of creative expression.

Strive to make your sexual encounters acts of love. Every act of physical sexuality should be expressed with love and kindness. Every act should be a form of giving as well as taking. When you acknowledge the role of spirit in sexuality, you shall begin to experience sexuality on a higher level. It will take on a higher vibration. It will be more intense. It will be more fulfilling, emotionally, physically and spiritually.

Your sexual expression is an integral aspect of who you are. Every act of your life which involved sex and/or love has made you, in a small way, who you are.

Love and Lust

It is important, therefore, that you integrate the force of love in your sexual acts. Allow this force to come into your being and to guide you. Allow this loving force to help you love others in a way which is not destructive. Love in a way which spreads love and joy instead of fear and disease.

When you kiss someone, kiss them with love. When you touch someone, touch them with love. When you hold someone, hold them with love.

Q: *Is there any connection between sex, guilt and disease?*

A: Guilt is one of the greatest root causes of disease. Guilt is one of the greatest killers of the human spirit. If you are actively incorporating guilt in your life, you are taking on a very powerful and destructive force. Say good-bye to guilt.

Q: *Are we really meant to be monogamous as a species?*

A: You are meant to love one another. Problems arise because love is not the motivating factor behind most sexual encounters. Love is not the motivating force behind monogamy. People are motivated to be monogamous by fear, jealousy, power and control. If sexual expression was always motivated by love, there would be no such thing as monogamy. If everyone truly loved everyone else, sexual expression would simply be a reflection of the love we feel for each-other. However that is not the way things are.

The Risk and Reunion of Marriage

Marriage is a learning and growing experience. Through marriage you come to know yourself better. In committing yourself to another, you are able to commit to yourself. In committing to one another, you commit to a greater whole. This wholeness is what marriage is all about.

In your day and age, there is struggle away from wholeness. There is a struggle to maintain separate identities. You strive to maintain independence. Independence and true commitment are not mutually exclusive. Independence and commitment go hand in hand. You cannot make a commitment to another unless you are committed to yourself. You must first establish your own independence and understand yourself. Once this has been accomplished then you can make a true commitment to another. The commitment to the other can be a many splendored thing. For in the commitment to the other, you continue to learn about yourself.

Marriage is the desire of two souls to create a reunion of the spirit. On a spiritual level you are always connected to each other. Yet on the physical level, you often fail to feel this connection. You use your physical bodies and your world of matter to increase your feelings of separateness. Through marriage, you have the opportunity to really experience your connectedness. As you struggle toward intimacy with each other, you struggle towards intimacy with yourself. As you move toward this holy state of intimacy, you will discover the reunion of spirit. The union of spirit is the natural state of interconnectedness that exists between all forms of life.

Problems can arise in your marital state when you view this reunion as the end of experience. Your marriage should be the beginning of your desire to grow. Once you have experienced the reunion of the spirit in marriage, your spirit longs to recreate that experience. The experience of reunion can be recreated in many non-threatening ways. It is essential for you to continue the process of growing and expanding your consciousness. Your marriage should not restrict you from doing this.

Your marriages are living and vibrant institutions. They are energy exchanges. Your relationships are malleable. They are involved in the ebb and flow of life. Your relationships are not static. They are live organisms. They need to be fed and nurtured. You need to understand what kind of nourishment your marriage needs. Actively involve yourself in creating that nourishment.

You are not alone in your endeavors. Throughout the world, there are individuals who are trying to create relationships which are alive. Your marriage is alive. It has a life of its own. It is longing to express itself. Do not smother your marriage. Do not allow it to smother you. Recognize that it needs to express, develop and grow. It needs to rediscover itself. It needs to reignite itself on a regular basis.

When your marriage is stimulated you may feel threatened. It is natural to feel threatened when someone or something you love changes. You feel the risk of loss. This fear of loss keeps you down. You want to maintain the status quo. You want to protect yourself. Yet you protect yourself at the expense of your own personal growth. When you involve yourself in the state of marriage, you take a risk. In taking risks you expand your awareness and grow as a human being. Risks are made to be taken.

To make a marriage is to make a commitment. Commitment is important. It is important because it involves a structuring of your value system. You cannot make a commitment unless you have thought about your values. Commitment is simply an assessment of one's values. Values need to be assessed. If at some point your value structure changes, you run the risk that your commitment will change as well.

A change in values is often a change in commitments. It is essential, therefore, that you allow yourself the flexibility to deal with change. You need flexibility for the changing roles you play in each other's lives. Flexibility is one of the keys to making your life work. There are times when you need to bend and times when you need to flow. There are times when you need to let go. There are times when you need to hold on with all your might.

In your world there is no security, other than the security you find within yourself. Those of you who turn to marriage to find security may be rudely awakened. Your marriage can only be as secure as you are. Do not turn to another to find what lies within you.

Your partners can be your props in the wind. Your partners can help to sustain you during times of sadness and sorrow. Yet your true anchor in the storm shall be your own soul. Your soul is your own best friend. Yet it longs to reconnect with other souls. Therefore, in entering a state of marriage, you are allowing your soul to come a little closer to home.

Estrangement: Opportunity for Reunion

E strangement involves a separation between two individuals. The separation may be physical, spiritual, intellectual, or emotional. Separation always occurs for a reason. Often the reason is unclear at first.

Two individuals come together and experience a tremendous amount of intensity. When this togetherness occurs, there is the surrender of the individual ego identity. Something clicks—the souls become united. During these moments of intensity, a tremendous amount of learning and sharing takes place. One individual becomes a part of the other. The person becomes "a part of your life."

When an individual becomes a part of your life, you have responsibility towards that individual. Responsibility means caring enough about the other individual to allow for a continuing sense of intimacy. Intimacy is the sharing of deep aspects of one another's lives. With intimacy there comes responsibility. Accepting responsibility means that at some point you may need to sacrifice your own individual needs or desires to further the advancement of the other individual or the couple. When you put yourself in the position of having to sacrifice your own individual needs for those of another, you have attained a true and profound sense of intimacy.

There are times when it is frightening to accept this responsibility. It is frightening to accept responsibility for yourself. When you have made a soul connection with another, the obligation you have to the other person becomes the obligation you have to yourself. If you cannot rise above your own needs to meet the needs of another, you are unable to accept responsibility for caring for and loving yourself.

Estrangement is not always a separation between two separate individuals. It can be a separation from your own soul. When you push aside someone with whom you have been intimate, you are truly pushing aside an aspect of yourself.

Every separation which you have experienced in your life is an opportunity to come together again. Every separation that you experience gives you a golden opportunity to reunite with your soul. During moments of estrangement, your soul is speaking to you. Listen to it.

In your days to come there will be many opportunities to be reunited with those from whom you have been separated. You do not have to come together physically for a reunion to occur. You can forgive and heal yourselves on the spiritual level. Coming together following estrangement offers many opportunities for growth.

Q: *Is there something you can say to people who have lost someone they loved through the process of death?*

A: This lesson is essentially meant to deal with estrangements between individuals who are living and who have made a conscious choice to be apart. But you raise a good point—that the process of death can create a separation. There is not so much estrangement, in this case, as there is physical separation. In estrangement, there is a feeling of lack of connected-ness. In death there is a physical lack of connected-ness.

The soul of every individual who dies is alive. Most likely it is functioning at a much higher level than when it was housed in a physical body. The soul then, may be wandering for a time—searching for its next role in life. There may be the desire to be connected with those on the earth plane.

Although you exist on different planes of being you can still experience togetherness. This can be done by the practice of astral-projection. Through astral-projection the earth plane individual's soul can enjoy the company of the soul who has passed on. During astral-projection, you can experience the beautiful communion you had together on earth. You can even come closer in the spiritual sense. So those desirous of this closeness should open themselves up to such opportunity. You are never really apart. Once you have shared intimacy your energy is always a part of one another's.

The Favor of Rejection

Rejection is not rejection. It is the opportunity to begin anew. It is an opportunity to approach life in a new way. You experience rejection as the lack of acceptance of an aspect of yourself. You seek the approval of others. Yet feelings of rejection stem from ones lack of approval of self.

Rejection allows you to come to an understanding of your insecurities. Put them on a platter and examine them. Look at the aspect of yourself which you feel was rejected. Examine its quality. Do *you* really believe that the quality of the aspect needs some improvement? If so, you have the opportunity to strengthen the perceived weakness. Perhaps there is no need for improvement. Then believe in yourself.

Rejection is an opportunity for you to examine yourself. Look at the private side, the insecure side, the side you do not allow the public to see. Face your insecurity. Face your fear. Then find a way to alleviate both.

One way to alleviate fear and insecurity is to begin the process of self-affirmation. Frame a positive statement of how you would like to see yourself, and repeat it daily in your meditations.

Rejection is simply an eye-opener. It is an opportunity for you to be your own best friend. Be your greatest fan! Blow your trumpet and herald your accomplishments. You only experience rejection if you reject yourself.

You give power and control to another individual if you allow their rejection to affect you. This is a very common form of manipulation in your society. You can see this process at work in battering relationships between men and women. The batterer continuously rejects his partner. The partner forms an image of herself as worthless. This same manipulative process takes place in many areas of life. Many times we allow others to form our images of who we are.

You must not allow external forces to control the way you feel about yourself. You must not allow other people's perceptions to define who you are. You are the master creator of yourself. Acts of rejection are really favors. They give you the opportunity to improve and/or affirm yourself.

Friendships:
Bridges to Knowledge

Your friends are your greatest teachers. Yet sometimes they irritate you beyond belief. Begin to take note of the things which cause you great irritation. Keep track of them. Write them down. Take notes. The things which irritate you are important. They offer you a lesson to learn.

Your irritations are mirrors for your own personal growth. If someone elses behavior irritates you—pay attention. Your friend acts as a mirror to reflect your own issue back to you. Why is it that you allow a particular mode of behavior to affect you? Do you also sometimes act in the same offensive fashion? Perhaps you need to change your own behavior or response.

Do not assume that if somebody is doing something which irritates you that it is solely a personal issue. Often there is an issue which needs to be worked out with the individual friend. You draw to you friendships which will allow you to experience intense learning. When we learn to communicate truthfully, we grow.

Individuals often feel responsible for the feelings and behavior of others. Although the conduct of others is always connected to you in some way, you are not responsible for the feelings and behavior of others. Each individual determines how they will allow others to affect them.

Friendships are important for self-growth. Pay attention to your friendships. Learn from the lessons they seek to teach you. Developing a friendship should be a conscious process. When you need a friend do not reach out and grab the first person available. Think about what you need. Think about who can best fulfill your need. Relationships should not be treated in a haphazard way. Relationships are designed to be your bridges to knowledge.

Your relationships are your responsibilities. Yet the most important relationship that you have is your relationship to yourself. Why is it that we cannot have relationships with others that are continuous and placid? Because the relationship that we have with ourselves is never particularly placid. There are always aspects to ourselves which we don't like. The friendships that we develop mirror to us those aspects of ourselves. We then can consciously try to change our own behavior.

Q: *I've recently been working with a person who sometimes makes me very angry. I feel a great sense of injustice when he gets all macho and uses himself in an aggressive fashion. I have a very strong reaction to it. I don't believe in using force with people. Are you saying that perhaps I don't deal with my own aggression very well?*

A: The issue of aggressiveness has been raised in your life. It is up to you to try and understand why this particular issue is of relevance to you. Why do you give him power over you? Are there aspects of yourself which deal with others in this way? Do you condemn that kind of behavior? Look at your fears, your judgments. You may need to develop courage so that you are not intimidated by others who treat you this way. You may need to develop tolerance so that you can understand the pain that would make an individual treat others in this way.

Q: *It just seems to me that it's not a mistake to judge somebody who's putting people down in a very negative fashion. I feel that it makes sense for me to judge that and to try and prevent it.*

A: This individual needs to learn a lesson of some kind. It is not wrong for him to go through the lessons that he needs to learn. This is how he develops himself in a better way. To that extent his behavior is not wrong and it is not for you to judge it. This does not mean that you should not help this person to learn his lessons. In allowing him to learn these lessons, you are aiding the universe. If you would allow yourself to teach this person instead of condemning him, it would benefit everyone.

Labor of Love

L abor is the exercise of the human mind or body. It is the productive use of your talent, creativity and mental ability. Through your labors you experience being.

Your labors produce products. They achieve goals. You experience cause and effect in action. You see results. Yet your labors bring you benefits that go beyond the physical.

Every cell in your body and mind contains creative ability. These abilities have a deep need for self-expression. You exercise your physical body to keep it in good shape. Your mental and creative aspects are in need of exercise as well. When you exercise your creative and mental aspects you express yourself. You emit emotion and passion. The expression of these emotions makes the world a better place to be.

Therefore, exercise your mind, your heart and your soul. Create a living for yourself. There is a direct result between the output of creative labor, and the input of materialistic joy. Reap the results of your labors. When you receive material pleasure, you are receiving a gift from the universe for the labor you have performed.

Your work is a major aspect of your identity. Individuals often define themselves by their occupations. Their work becomes who they are. Therefore, what you choose to do is what you choose to call yourself. Your occupation is a significant aspect of your being. Many hours and years of your life are spent working. It is therefore essential that you choose to perform a labor which will give you the identity you desire. Your work is a major aspect of who you are.

Envision yourself engaging in the line of work of your choice. Envision yourself being productive. Envision those around you supporting you in this line of work. Envision everyone rejoicing at your success.

Every tree, flower and butterfly has its position in the universal scheme of things. Every element of nature has its role to play. When the roles are working harmoniously the sound is melodious.

Find this melody in your own life. Find your niche in the scheme of things. Create harmony in your environment. The harmony which you create will carry forth a harmonic melody into the far-reaching forests of the world.

Your labors are not distinct from your pleasures. Your labors take place in a playground. Your labors are a wondrous, integrated, expression of self. Working need not be drudgery. Whistle while you work.

Your work is your opportunity to thank the world for your existence. The world does not owe you a living. You owe "living" to the world. Perceive of your labors as the rent you pay for having the opportunity to experience life on this planet. Fill your labors with love! The mountains, the seaside, the canyons are all put here for your pleasure. They are put here to bring you peace and serenity to which you are entitled. Give back a labor of love.

On Finding Balance: Families, Addiction, Work and Intimacy

Lures are the things which entice you. Lures dangle in front of you. A part of you reaches out to touch, yet another aspect of your being holds you back. When you hear the term "lure," you may think of the things in your life which have been defined by others as "sins." You think of drugs, alcohol, and extramarital sex. You think of gambling, lying and other such activities. These are not the only lures which exist in your lives. The most enticing yet elusive lures are love, peace and spiritual awareness.

Each of you is being lured at this very moment. You are being lured by the positive forces which surround you. You must make choices. You make choices between things which are seemingly "good" and seemingly "bad." You battle between right and wrong. How do you know which way to turn? Should you trust a lure with glamour? Should you trust a lure with intensity? Or should you trust the lure which is boring, for in boredom there is safety?

You would like to achieve many things in your life. You would like to achieve personal happiness and financial success. You would like to have good, strong, loving relationships. You would like to be well known for your intelligence. Life seems to dictate sacrifice. In order to have an extraordinary career, one finds herself neglecting the personal side of life. To have a good, strong family life, one doesn't put in the hours at the job which are necessary to have a sterling career. How then, can you ever maintain a balance? How can you choose between the things that lure you? Is it necessary for you to choose at all?

Each of you deserves fulfillment on all levels of your being. It is not necessary for you to choose between your personal and professional success. As you study metaphysics and increase your awareness, you shall be given many tools which can aid you in the division of your energies.

Behind every lure there is a learning. It is necessary for you to develop a consciousness about your choices. Roads in your life which appear destructive, such as alcoholism, may appear as a way to *give* you a sense of control. You can control your own life. You determine your destiny.

If you are lured down a destructive path, be aware of your power to overcome. Do not despair if you find yourself involved in addictive behavior. Do not despair if you find yourself involved in destructive realationships. Through these lures, you have the opportunity to discover your own inner power. When you touch this power, you can use it to create balance in your being. You are given the opportunity to satisfy your emotional, intellectual and spiritual needs from within.

At some time in your life, you involve yourself in a familial relationship. You are either born into a family, or you raise a family of your own. The relationships which you develop in your family, whether as a child, or as an adult, are extremely important. Pay attention to them.

Your relatives are significant people. They will give you the opportunity to learn many lessons.

Often there is tremendous friction between family members. This friction has a root cause. Each friction arises out of a recognition that all souls were once one. Each soul leads a separate life in this physical existence. This brings upon you tremendous frustration and pain. There is the recognition of the oneness and divinity that once existed. There is also the painful awareness of the physical separateness of each of you in this life. Recognize the soul connection between your family members.

Your family members will abide by you, in times when others will not. Your family members will often remain loyal in times of trouble. Your family members are your soul brothers and sisters.

You may not feel the closeness that you expect to feel in your family relationship. Your family members are brought together for a reason. You offer each other opportunities for continued learning and growth.

As you feel the pain, stress and anxiety which exists in many of your family units, recognize that the pain stems from love. For it is only where there is recognition of the oneness of all life that there can be sorrow in the awareness of separation.

Your family relationships ebb and flow. Your family members can abide by you, or blow away in the wind. Give your family attention, energy and love. In family life, you have the opportunity to come a little closer to home. You have the opportunity to spend years of time growing close together. The mere gift of the time gives you the opportunity to develop intimacy.

Intimacy is the key to connecting with the soul. Intimacy brings you closer to oneness. Give intimacy the opportunity to surface in your family relationships.

Many individuals fear intimacy. The fear of intimacy is really the fear of coming to know and understand self. It is only when you truly open up to another that you are able to see yourself. In the act of opening up and exposing yourself to another human being you can embrace your own soul.

Family life is being shattered in many ways. One such way is the diversion of energy into working for a living. Working often leaves you feeling bedraggled. You come home with little time and energy to spend with your family. The nature of your work life depletes your precious resources. Begin to restructure the way you think about your work. Many of you allow your jobs to take control of you. Instead, take control of your jobs.

You have the power to create and control your own work life. Do not leave it up to others to provide a function for you in life. You can create work opportunities which will fit naturally and peacefully into your home lives. You can create options which would allow you to spend less time at work and more time at home. This should not only be encouraged for the women in your culture. Both men and women need to focus more of their energy on interpersonal relationships.

Do not be a slave at your work place. Do not allow others to decide things for you. It may be difficult to change the dynamics at first. Yet by beginning to change the way you think about your work, you can begin to make your work work for you. There is power in collective action.

There is power in collective thought. You need to discuss your concerns about your work life with your co-workers. You need to develop working schedules that are flexible, and allow you to spend more quality time with your family. This is a goal that is desired by many members of your workforce. It is simply a matter of getting people to talk. Then you can follow up with action.

A loving co-existence can develop between one's home life and one's professional life. They can nurture each other. There need not be this tremendous separation between one's family life and one's employment. Begin to design in your mind the kind of life that would meet all your needs. First comes the dream, next the reality.

The New Age is coming upon you. It is an opportunity for you to restructure all aspects of your existence. There needs to be a significant change in the workplace. There needs to be a decision-making process whereby people, through their collective wisdom and judgment, can begin to take control of their own work lives.

This process begins at home. It begins in your daily meditations. Envision the balance between work life and family life. The two can co-exist harmoniously. They can co-exist in a way which is benefits individuals and society.

Work life and family life are beginning to merge. They must merge for you to carry on into the New Age. You will then feel peaceful, instead of harried and full of stress. Stress is the number one killer of human life. Stress can be conquered by working together to create a system where there is a balance between work and play.

The concept of family needs to be extended. Your neighbors are your family. Your friends are your family. Many members of your community have mutual needs. Yet there is a strong emphasis placed on individuals taking care of their own problems. Join forces to meet eachother's needs. When you join forces, you increase your effectiveness. You create solutions for yourselves. The solutions are in your own hearts and minds. The solutions are waiting to be born. Recognize that you are one and the same with your neighbor. When you gain this understanding you will be much closer to eliminating your present problems.

Q: *Are you saying that if we are lured down a seemingly destructive path, that we still might be on the right track?*

A: That's correct. You may find yourself down and out if you allow yourself to be lured by a destructive force. But in the destruction, there is the opportunity to rebuild. Through destruction, there is the coming in touch with strength. The individual has the opportunity to conquer the source of her downfall. Often lures are placed to take us down a so-called wrong path. Then we can rediscover our innate ability to overcome our problems.

Soul Food For Thought

Food is organic in nature. The organisms which are contained in food are alive. The food which you ingest is living material. It gives you the continuation of physical life. It also gives you great pleasure. Yet food is not simply the means by which you sustain yourself.

Food is also symbolic. World problems are often discussed over the breaking of bread. Your social life revolves around food. Your work day revolves around mealtimes. Food is a central focus of your life. How is it that the role of food takes on such importance?

Each of you desires self-fulfillment. Your image of fulfillment comes from the notion of having a full belly. Wholesome nourishment is fulfilling. A person who has eaten a wondrous meal is deemed to be fulfilled. Imagine the moments following Thanksgiving dinner at your grandmother's house. You're rubbing your belly and kicking back in the overstuffed chair. This is a moment of contentment and happiness. These are the moments that you desire to recreate in your life. You continue to eat food attempting to attain the "image" of fulfillment. You eat in an attempt to nourish your soul.

Your body is the temple of your soul. Before you engage in eating behaviors which are compulsive, recognize that it is not your body which is seeking nourishment. It is your soul. When you understand that it is the soul that is in need, you can change your behavioral pattern. Begin the process of replenishing your soul instead of merely increasing your caloric intake.

Eating good food can help to replenish the soul. The food you eat should have a wholesome and nourishing quality. If you focus on eating these particular kinds of food, you will find that your body has been nourished. In nourishing your body, you nourish your soul.

It is important to focus upon whole grain foods. For in the "whole" of the grain, there is the "whole-someness" of nourishment. When you strip the grain of its natural property, you strip it of its ability to nourish your body. Thus you strip your body of the ability to provide a safe and secure home for your soul.

Food draws you together. It gives you the opportunity to to exchange company. The true meaning of the coming together, of the breaking of the bread, is the coming together of the souls. The food should not be the focal point of your dinners. Food is the magnet that draws you into each other's presence. Then you can share your souls. The sharing of food is the sharing of energy. Food is a wonderful containment of energy. The ingestion of food is the ingestion of energy.

Energize what you eat. It is customary to say a prayer before one eats. You bless the food for its intended use. Begin this practice if you have lost the custom. When you bless the food, it is actually blessed. The food receives divine energy from your oral blessing. When you bless your food, you are giving it the positive energy it needs to nourish your soul. You overlook the "soul" aspect of eating. Food can nourish the body without this blessing. The blessing is intended to help the food nourish the *soul*.

The preparation of food is a creative act of love. The reason home-cooked food tastes so good is because it has been cooked with love. When you are preparing a meal, prepare it with love. The ingredient which is missing from the pages of your cookbooks, is the ingredient of love. When you create your meals, consciously incorporate a cup of love into each dish. Write this ingredient on the recipe card. When you pass on the recipe you spread a little love.

There are many important lessons to be learned from the art of cooking. Cooking is an incredible experience because it allows you to take a variety of ingredients and mix them together to create a magical potion. The ingredients of your being can be recombined to create a new you as well. Your being is actually the combination of a multitude of separate ingredients. They can be varied in the same way that a recipe can be varied. You delight in trying out a new recipe. You can delight in trying out a new you as well. Work on developing a different characteristic of your being every day.

Your food is your companion on your voyage home. Your food is longing for you to recognize that it is alive. When you ingest food, you are essentially "taking" its life by allowing its properties to change. You give it a new life. Recognize that the food is making a sacrifice for your benefit. It enjoys playing this role in your life. Yet it would like an acknowledgement. The acknowledgement, as previously mentioned, can be given in the form of a blessing.

Recognize the plight of your farmers. The farmers have dedicated their entire existence to providing you and your family with nourishment. In the hearts, minds and souls of these individuals, there exists a consciousness which celebrates the union between humanity and nature.There is an understanding of the role that nature plays in the creation of your food. There is an understanding that the food which grows from the earth is a bounty from the world above. The crops which are raised by the farmers are truly a gift from Mother Nature. To honor this gift, bless Mother Nature. Acknowledge the role that nature plays in sustaining your life as a human being.

You face a world in which you cannot exist without food. You have made yourselves dependent on the earth. Recognize the interdependence you have with the earth. Your individual soul is intertwined with the soul planet. You require the earth's land to produce the source of your nourishment. When you come to truly understand this interdependence you will create a harmonious partnership with nature.

Q: *Many people these days suffer from eating disorders. Some people binge on food and others starve themselves. What is at the root of these illnesses?*

A: These particular illnesses seem to affect the female species more than the male species. Your social science observers characterize this occurrence as being a result of fashion consciousness. The root is really much deeper. The women who suffer from these disorders are strongly connected with nature on the soul level. The earth-bound level of their being experiences the separation from nature in a most acute way. The "lower self" feels abandoned, in much the same way a child would feel upon being abandoned by her mother. The desire to overeat compulsively is really a desire to become one with the Mother Nature spirit. Food is the gift of Mother Nature. Therefore women turn to food in an attempt to find the loving sustenance of Mother Nature. Of course binging only results in illness. Food should be respected and blessed for its intended use. Then nourishment will be experienced.

The opposite of over-indulgence is near starvation. This behavior pattern also acknowledges the separation from nature. The fear and hurt of the separation is remembered and felt. Starvation is defensive behavior. It seeks to prevent a union with Mother Nature. Then there is no threat of having to re-experience the pain of separation.

People who suffer from these disorders need to align themselves with their higher being. They need to seek alignment with Mother Nature. As they develop themselves spiritually they will find that he emptiness which led to their behavior will disappear. When the emptiness disappears the behavior disappears.

Nature's Vibrational State

Nature is alive and well. Nature is desirous of working with you on your path towards enlightenment. Nature is desirous of being your teacher and your friend.

You have often abused nature. At all times you have stripped nature to its core. You have killed it. It is time to change.

Begin communicating with the nature that surrounds you. Understand that nature has a movement. You have something to learn from that movement. You, as well as nature, are connected to the universal scheme of things.

There are moments when glaciers slide and take away human life. There are times when volcanoes erupt and people die. There are moments when nature creates storms and kills your crops. Yet nature also creates the rainfall and the sunshine which is needed to grow your food. You and nature are intimately intertwined. You and nature are one and the same.

Your scientists are learning ways to control nature. You plant your clouds with seeds to produce rain. You create artificial sunshine. You are learning to use physical means to control the forces of nature. Nature cannot be controlled if you continue to view it as your enemy. Nature is willing to work with you. View it as your companion in your endeavors towards spiritual understanding.

The trees, the air, the wind, the rocks and the sea are alive. They are alive in a sense to which you have not yet awakened. They consist of a molecular structure which is very much like your own. You are made of matter. Every other form of existence can be transformed into matter. The matter which makes up the elements of nature is the same matter of which you are made.

Develop an alignment between the matter within you, and the matter within the forces of nature. Recognize that you are not made solely of matter. You are made of gases. You are made of light. You are made of liquid. The gas, liquid and light forms of which you are made, are the same forms which make up the elements of nature.

You have advanced to a state where you can understand the elements of which you are made. You do this through your mental capacity. Nature has long been aware of the material of which it is made. Nature becomes aware of this knowledge by tuning into vibrational energy. In this way it can receive and condense knowledge. Knowledge is received by nature through a molecular structure similar to the one that processes your feelings.

Nature is aware of its "alive" consciousness. Awaken to that consciousness. You have the capacity to commune with nature. You seek the solitude and solace of the surroundings of nature. You turn to the land, the fields, and the streams to collect your thoughts. Nature puts you in touch with who you are. You are nature. You a part of all that exists in nature. All that exists in nature is a part of you.

You are being beckoned by nature to develop an understanding of the ways you can work together to heighten the awareness of life on your planet. When you are lying in the grass, perceive of the grass as a live form of consciousness. Receive knowledge, love and energy from the grass. When you are lying on the beach, feel the rays of sunshine touching your body. They are not simply giving you a tan. You are receiving knowledge, understanding and love from this tremendous source of light. When you are up to your neck in dirt and mud, recognize that the molecules within this substance possess a certain historic knowledge of the way of the world. Children who love to get dirty are in touch with a simple understanding. When they cover themselves with dirt, they are covering themselves with life.

When you observe the branches of a tree moving, recognize that this tree is waving to you. The sway of the branches express the spirit of the tree. It is an interaction between the spirit of the wind and the spirit of the tree. There is a dance occurring. You dance with friends for entertainment. The trees and the wind dance together.

As human beings you have your moments of rage. The consciousness of nature has its frustrations as well. There is often a calm before the storm. The calm before the storm is your opportunity to develop communion with nature so that the storm will not occur.

You live your life on this plane in total ignorance of the spirit which exists within your plant, animal and mineral kingdoms. You live your life in ignorance of the interconnectedness which exists between each of these spheres of reality. You are not alone as a species on your earth. Numerous other forms of consciousness are existent here. They are alive. Awaken to these new-found friends.

There is no reason for you to feel lonely when you are living in the midst of loving consciousness. Tune into the vibrational state of the earth and all its inhabitants. Nature is awaiting you with open arms.

The clouds in the sky have long enjoyed changing formations for your visual pleasure. They now await the opportunity to bring you pleasure in new-found ways. They are awaiting the opportunity to fill your heart and fill your soul with their consciousness, their knowledge, and their love. They are asking you to perceive of them as guests, as company upon your plane. They are not separate and distinct from you. They are a part of your awareness. They are a part of your consciousness. You are one with the kingdom of nature.

Crime Does Pay

In your society there is a rampant epidemic of criminal activity. Why is crime permitted to exist? Why does the media focus on such behavior? Criminal conduct has its root in the desire of the soul to learn and to be recognized. Crime gives you an opportunity to think about your laws and mores.

Your society invents laws. Laws are meant to proscribe behavior. Laws are meant to keep you under control. The individual who is willing to break the societal rules is an unusual individual indeed. This individual breaks out of a prision of sorts. He expresses himself freely, without regard for societal approval.

The desire to act against the government, against religious mores, or against ones parents is one method of individual growth. Breaking the rules gives one a sense of identity. To break with tradition and to commit a crime is an exercise of independence. However, society has determined that certain kinds of expression are not healthy for the rest of society. Criminal activity affects everyone. Everyone has the opportunity to learn and grow from criminal conduct.

Criminals are great teachers. They push you to think about your values in life. Their conduct raises issues of life, death, freedom, captivity, security and fear. They force you to think about questions of trust, honor and integrity.

143

SOJOURNS OF THE SOUL

The criminal also has an opportunity to learn from his experience. It is called jail. When you put your people behind bars, you give them the opportunity to think. You give them time to meditate. You give them time for self-reflection.

As your criminals sit in jail, you too have time to think. You are busy with your legislators passing additional laws to inhibit and repress conduct. You cry out, "How can we not have laws? If we did not have laws which punished criminal conduct there would be utter chaos on earth." Strive for a world in which laws are not necessary. A world in which individuals have respect for the life of others. A world in which all individuals live in abundance and fulfillment. Then criminal conduct would not be necessary.

Criminal behavior raises the question of punishment. The punishment you inflict upon convicted criminals is not the real punishment they will suffer. The real punishment is self- punishment. It is the way they come to perceive themselves. They feel rejection from your society. They perceive of themselves as rejects. They then become rejects. The true punishment is not the deprivation of freedom. The true punishment comes from believing that one is not a useful and productive member of society. One becomes what one destines oneself to be.

Crime is looked upon as a problem. Crime is a problem if you do not allow yourselves to listen to and learn from those who rebel against society. Criminal conduct expresses the desire to be set free. Free from socially ordained constrictions on behavior. Criminals are screaming out. They want to be recognized for who they are. They feel powerless. And so they take their power in the only way they know how.

In your society there is a tremendous amount of

violent criminal conduct. Violence is an accepted part of your culture. Violence is accepted in the ways that families discipline their children. Violence is accepted in the sporting arena. Violence is accepted in war. By accepting violence in your culture in one way, you condone the existence of violence in other ways.

If you would like to rid violence from your society, you need to begin to eradictate it from the most personal areas of your life. You need to treat your children with love and respect. Do not hit them with your hands and broomsticks. You need to disapprove of violence in your sporting arena. Simply allow good fun and games to take place. You need to stop killing each other on your street corners, in your prisons, and on your battlefields.

Killing in "acceptable" ways gives the notion that such activity is an approved form of expression. Violence is a form of expression. It is a primitive form. Individuals turn to expressing their feelings through violent means when they are unable to express themselves in any other way.

To eliminate crime and violent behavior, you need to allow individuals to express themselves freely. They need to receive validation for self-expression at a very young age. A sense of human dignity should be afforded to everyone who thinks in a different way.

Human behavior needs to be changed. You need to allow love to flow through the systems where you are desiring to rehabilitate. If you continue to treat the incarcerated with violence and deprivation, you continue to exacerbate the vicious cycle. You cannot teach people to love by hating them. Love thy enemy as thyself.

Q: *Some people need to be locked up to protect others. How can we get society to accept another form of "punishment?"*

A: Your society is intent on punishing. Your society focuses on retribution. It seems virtually impossible to get people to love the individuals whom they despise the most. Yet the biggest enemy lurks in your own heart. It is fear. You fear these individuals. It is hard to love what you fear. You must try to see the God in everyone. And you must see the "criminal element" within yourself. You are a part of one another. When you fear the criminal you fear yourself. It is your own fears which need to be worked on.

Terrorism:
Fear As The Captor

Terrorism is a frightening phenomenon. Terrorist acts do not appear to be rational. The victims of terrorism have seemingly done no harm to their terrorists. Terrorism springs up unexpectedly. The unexpected, random qualities of terrorisim make it frightening. They are also the aspects which make it most effective.

Fear makes terrorism effective. The terrorist cannot be effective unless he has a fearful prey. You have made yourselves that fearful prey. You are susceptible to terrorism because of your fear and insecurity. You have brought terrorism upon yourselves by perceiving of yourselves as separate from those who terrorize you. You fail to see what you have in common. Your fears are really your captors. If you had no fear of terrorism, it would wipe itself out. A country that has no fear does not find it necessary to murder others.

Your acts of bombing are not acts of strength. You cannot stamp out terrorism through force. True strength does not come from bombs. True strength comes from inner wisdom. True strength comes from a recognition that you are one with all of God's creation. You are God's creation. The individuals who inhabit every country of the world are God's creation.

Through your struggles with each other you seek to

know and understand yourselves better. Through your brutality you seek to learn about yourselves. Your desire to stamp out terrorism is really a desire to stamp out the aspect of yourself which is fearful. You hope to eradicate fear from your heart. Yet you do not look to the true source of your fear. Instead, you objectify your fears onto something external.

Your fear does not exist because terrorism exists. Your fear exists as an act of self-hatred. When you insist upon the destruction the human beings, no matter what form it may take, you insist upon diminishing your own God essence. Do not seek to destroy this God essence. Bless it, expand it, and allow it to fill your earth.

How can you actively work for peace on your earth? Meditate upon the creation of a peaceful and loving world. Visualize a land without barries. Create a world consciousness. You are the world. You cohabit this planet. You are here to learn about sharing. You are here to grow towards oneness.

To experience oneness with the universe, experience oneness on your planet. You are brothers and sisters. You have far more in common than you know. Your world struggles with war, terrorism, and division among nations. This struggle has a purpose.

Wars will eventually be the process through which you will unify yourselves. As you struggle with each other, you lay the ground work for coming together again. As you create division by wars and political schemes, you lay the groundwork for spiritual union. Devastation will arise in your world following war. This devastation will create a readiness for spiritual awakening.

Turmoil is a part of growth. All chaos, pain and suffering is the root of spiritual awakening. You have heard the expression "suffering is good for the soul." Suffering allows the soul to traverse through pain, so that it can awaken to the light of higher consciousness. Through sorrow and suffering, you enlighten yourselves. There is a better way for the world to exist.

Have faith. The sun rises over the mountain tops every morning. Do not fear that in your silliness you will destroy your planet. Your planet is experiencing a tremendous influx of spiritual energy. The power of the spirit is much stronger than the power of the bomb.

Q: *Throughout these sessions you have said that we don't need to suffer to get what we want. Isn't it a contradiction to say that we must suffer to achieve enlightenment?*

A: You are right. There is an apparent contradiction. The words which mandate that you suffer should be deleted. Suffering is not mandated . There are those, however, who will find it necessary to suffer. All knowingness is arrived at through experience.

Those who experience an expansive view of life educate their souls. So it is not that you must suffer, but that you may choose to suffer. There are those of you who have suffered enough. When you have learned the necessary lessons, you will release yourselves from the suffering. Only you can make that determination. So many of you do not feel as though you have suffered enough. Ask yourself that question at this very moment. Have you suffered enough? Many of you will respond with a resounding "no." You want to punish yourselves. You don't love yourselves enough. These lessons are an attempt to get you to realize the ways in which you unconsciously create your lives. When you become aware of your unconscious powers of creation, you can change your lives.

149

Pollution is a Spiritual Problem: A Lesson from the Star Sirius

The stars in your universe are actually homes. They are the homes of beings of light. These beings care deeply for you. They are desirous of making contact with you, to aid you in your spiritual journeys.

Welcome to the star system Sirius. The star Sirius is the home of the "Great White Brotherhood/Sisterhood." This order is a collective consciousness. The members of this Brotherhood/Sisterhood work closely with individuals on your earth to raise the level of consciousness.

Brother Jove is a member of this order. He seeks to make you aware of the problem pollution poses in the development of spiritual awareness. Pollution stands to block the communication between the earth and celestial bodies.

JOVE:

An energy field encircles your planet. It creates the powerful sensation of fog. It cloaks your earth with density. It is helping to prevent the filtering of knowledge between our plane and yours. This energy field is pollution.

This pollution exists in your minds as well as your skies. Your minds are the creators of this pollution. It is your disrespect for life that allows such pollution to occur.

Pollution is a desire to self-destruct. Pollution is an expression of the lower aspects of your being. These aspects create a dense energy mass to try to keep you down. Pollution blinds you so that you cannot see the heavens. Pollution blinds you so that you cannot see the light.

Pollution is more than a political problem. Pollution is more than an ecological problem. Pollution is a spiritual problem.

Pollution manifests a desire to control the earth from the ground. It locks you into looking upon your earth as a place which needs to be saved. Pollution keeps you earth-bound. It keeps your energies focused on the material plane.

Your skies are riddled with smoke. You cannot see the heavens clearly. You love the earth. You must fight for the earth. Put your energies into the prevention of pollution. Yet look beyond the pollution. Clear the skies to receive our communications.

Fight with all your hearts and souls to stop the pollution which is engulfing your planet. Stop mistreatment of the energy fields which surround you. Recognize that within every tree, every rock and every bird that flies there is the essence of you. You are destroying that essence with your chemicals.

It is hoped your skies will begin to clear. It is hoped that your scientists will begin to look to the heavenly bodies for their guidance and knowledge. Then each of you shall come a little closer home.

Race: Distinction Without a Difference

Race is a category you have used to separate your-selves from each other. Race gives you a distinction you can use to make yourselves feel superior or inferior to others. You have differing cultures. The color of your skin may be different. This is where the distinction ends.

Within each of you there exists divine consciousness. Racial friction keeps you separated from this conscious-ness. Race creates a dividing line. This dividing line keeps you separated from yourself. This dividing line keeps you separated from your brothers and sisters. It keeps you separated from your soul.

When your collective consciousness split from the original source it manifested in physical form. It became your earth. The initial division was so catastrophic that your consciousness continued to divide. Through your fear, self-judgment, and doubt, you continued to separate from each other.

Your fears overcame you. Your division began to in-crease. You created new ways to separate yourselves from eachother. Your consciousness developed a way to look at an image of yourself, yet keep you apart from the source of that image. You created race. You created race as a means to alienate yourselves from each other. God consciousness knows no race.

When you feel racial prejudice, what you are really experiencing are your own fears of coming home to the ultimate source. You are really experiencing the fear of being consumed into one consciousness. You are continuing to divide yourself from your true home.

Align yourselves with other human beings. All human beings are essences of the original source of love and light. Maintain your individual cultures. Yet recognize that you are of the same consciousness.

Study cultures which are not your own. Learn about those who are unfamiliar to you. Do not reject people who look different. If you feel hatred when you are observing another individual, you are really seeing what you fear within yourself. Break down the barriers. In learning to accept the differences of others, you come to know yourself a little better.

Within each of you, you have all cultures. Within each of you, you are all races. Each of you contains all the memories of your previous incarnations. You have been all things.

You must recognize your equality with all humankind. Until each of you accepts your brothers and sisters of this planet as your true equals, you will continually be engaging in a struggle which keeps you separated from the original source.

This is your opportunity to overcome division. Carry the light high in your hands. You are longing to come home. Home is waiting for you with the hot fires burning, and with a pot of soup on the stove for your hungry soul. Home is beckoning you. Home is waiting for you, with a pillow to rest your head. Touch the heart and soul of a member of a different race. It will bring you a little closer to yourself. It will bring you a little closer to home.

Race: Distinction Without a Difference

Q: *Race is not the only factor people use to distinguish be-tween each other. Aren't differences positive?*

A: There are many different ways in which members of a society divide themselves from each other. You estab-lish class systems. There are the rich and there are the poor. You establish genders. There are men and women. You establish sexual orientations. There are homosexuals and heterosexuals. It's important that these differences exist. However, differences should be created out of love for individuality. Differences should not be created out of a need for divisiveness.

Money Magic

Y ou live in a physical world. You need to eat, sleep and clothe yourselves. For this you need money. Financial stability is not inconsistent with spiritual enlightenment.

Money is energy. You exchange it for other forms of energy. It is the power to create which is important, not the money itself. Acquiring material possessions will not make you happy. Experiencing abundance in all aspects of your life will.

You have devised various ways to create income for yourself. One such way is labor. Through your toil, the exertion of physical and mental energy, you receive financial gain. A second way to accumulate money is through inheritance. You can pass wealth from one generation to another. Thirdly, you can win money. You can be lucky and draw the magic numbers in a lottery. A fourth way to make money available is through the process of thievery. This method is looked down upon by your society. Yet there is another way to attain financial riches in your life. Develop a theory of abundance.

People focus upon money as a problem in their lives. Focusing on money as a problem creates the problem. You need to change your perspective on the issue of money. Do not perceive of yourself as in lack. Envision yourself in possession of the riches of the world. Attaining riches may simply mean having your freedom. Abundance allows you to make choices.

You have the power within you to create what you need to enjoy life. Concentrate on the means not just the end. Earning money is an act of creative expression. Focus on the creation. Enjoy the process!

Release the aspect of your consciousness which desires to possess. Possession depives others of freedom. If you possess something, you deprive yourself of freedom in the long run. When you draw the riches of the world to yourself, do it with a sense of freedom. All that you draw to you is free to return to the universe.

Your economic system functions under this theory. It is necessary for you to spend what you earn. If you did not spend the money you earn, your economic system would collapse. The universal economic system functions in much the same way.

The riches you attain are a gift from the universe. Utilize them. Then release them back to the universe. Never seek to keep them down. You cannot own them. When you seek to restrict the freedom of another form of matter, you give rise to a slave rebellion. All energy, whether in the material or ethereal form, desires to be free. It seeks to expand and explore the universe in its own way. Befriend your material possessions in the same way you would befriend any other individual. Do not possess them. Possessions have a life of their own.

Universal energy has an ebb and a flow. At times you experience the ebb. Many of you feel as though your life has been a gigantic ebb. You are waiting for the flow. The flow is within you. You have the power to turn on the faucet. You create the flow.

Q: *When you say you shouldn't seek to possess money - do you mean just amass it for its own sake?*

A: Physical possessions have a consciousness of their own. They are energy in a material form. When the

energy changes form, it will have a new consciousness. You cannot ever truly possess or control anything. Everything has a life of its own. Everything
seeks freedom in the same way that you seek to be
free. Your physical possessions are lent to you by the
universe. You cannot take them with you when you
leave. They will evolve into another existence once
their physical form disintegrates.

Q: *Aside from visualization, is there something else people
can do to experience more abundance?*

A: Channeled material is often criticized because it is
repetitive. It is repetitive because the human mind
needs repetition. It needs to hear things many times
from many different sources before it sinks in. Some
things bear repeating. The biggest block people have
in creating abundance is that they do not feel they are
worthy. Somehow they believe they are meant to
suffer. The crucial step which needs to be taken to
create abundance, is to believe with every cell of your
being that you are worthy. Affirm the divinity within
you. You are your own worst enemy. You must get
out of your own way. Perceive of yourself as being
worthy of an answer to your prayers.

Q: *If I visualize something that I really want for myself and
it doesn't come about, does that mean it is just not meant
to be, or does it mean I just wasn't visualizing in the
right way?*

A: There can actually be a conflict between your "physical" consciousness and your "soul" consciousness.
When you work in alignment with your "soul" consciousness, all you seek will be brought to you. Your
soul may be telling you, "You think that is what you

want, but truly it is not in your benefit in the long run." You may be visualizing with your "physical" self and that self may be in conflict with your "soul" self. Your "soul" self will always win. You need to align your "physical" and "soul" selves.

You may not be visualizing with the total essence of your being. You need to affirm with every cell of your being. You need to affirm with all your senses, your sight, your smell, your hearing, your touch. You need to wholeheartedly feel, touch, see, smell and experience what you desire to create. Every aspect of your being should be involved. It should not simply be a visualization. It should be an experiential moment wherein you create what you desire.

Q: *How about the starving people in Ethiopia? Are they starving because they don't see themselves as deserving?*

A: These situations are very difficult to explain to people on the physical plane. You have a value system which is based in physical reality. You view their starvation, pain, and suffering from a very physical perspective. You see them being denied the nourishment they need. There is an entirely different perspective to be gained by looking at this situation from a spiritual viewpoint.

In the Hindu culture there are individuals who consciously deprive themselves of food. They fast for long periods of time. They choose to do this with a conscious spiritual goal. Obviously the individuals who are starving in Ethiopia are not experiencing this same enlightenment. Their fasts are killing them. Yet, there is an aspect of their being which is spiritually evolving through the process of deprivation. When the physical body starves, the soul is nourished.

Conclusion:
The End Is The Beginning

Our journey is drawing to a close. What a marvelous journey it has been. We have explored many of the highways and byways of life. We hope that you have glimpsed that the paths of life extend far beyond the roads which pave your physical plane. You choose the direction your vehicle will travel. Forward movement is not always necessary for progress. You often go the farthest when you simply stand still.

You are an exact microcosm of the universe. All the knowledge of the universe exists within you. You are a tiny, encapsulated version of everything you perceive to be external. Look deep within yourself to learn the most valuable lessons of life.

We hope you have gained a new perspective from this journey. Did you take photographs? The images you have developed will be everlasting in your memory. The lessons you have learned will live on beyond this day. Incorporate them in the way you live your life. From time to time, flip through these pages. Pay attention to the place where your heart and eyes guide you. What may seem irrelevant and meaningless to you now, may be of paramount importance at some time in the future.

Experience life in the fullest of ways. Be aware of other dimensions of reality. You are not alone. A multitude of other life forms inhabit your universe. Consciousness is alive in your trees, your rocks and your stars in the sky.

You are conscious of your moments of togetherness. You fear the moment when you will be apart. You will never be separated from each other in an everlasting sense. There is a reunion coming. The reunion is a re-union of spirit. It is a reunion of all the loved ones from your past, present and future lives. We will all be to-gether again. There shall be cause for great celebration.

This reunion may be perceived to be light years away. Yet it takes place in the present moment. It occurs when we fully experience the inter-relatedness of all of our being. This inter- connection has never gone away. It will never go away. It is our intellect which prevents us from experiencing this oneness.

We are all one. We are one mind. We are one con-sciousness. That consciousness is seeking to resurface. That consciousness is seeking to awaken us to inter-dependence upon one another. At the same time it teaches us of our autonomy. We experience our separa-tion in order to increase our understanding of our oneness.

We thank each of you for taking the time out of your daily lives to experience these moments with us. We thank you for having the desire to know yourselves, and to know us better. Thank you for allowing us to learn from eachother. We hope that in the days and years to come you shall remember us. Remember our desire to love you. Remember our desire to be with you.

Spiritual love can fill your emptiness. You are more than a physical body. Do not ignore your spiritual self. We are your brothers. We are your sisters. We are your lovers. In the days and years to come we shall experience the reunion of which we have spoken. You shall recognize that we are familiar to each other. There are no strangers among us.

It has been some time since we have first created the words which appear upon these pages. Yet that time has been brief in comparison to the development of human time. Do not expect the changes in your life to be cataclysmic. Pay attention to subtlety. Pay attention to what appears just beyond the surface. It is there that you will find us cheering you on in your endeavors. It is there that we shall look for you for our own guidance and support.

A series of lectures by Raphael are available on cassette tape. For further information and a schedule of workshops and seminars please contact:

VOICES OF LIGHT
P.O. BOX 4630
Rolling Bay, WA.
98061-0630

Books and Products to help establish
The Global Spiritual Awakening

Kim D. Koenig was a criminal trial attorney for six years and was profiled in *Running form the Law* by Deborah Aaron.

In 1986, Kim Koenig's vision changed and she became a spiritual channeler. She co-founded *Voices of Light,* dedicated to bringing uplifting ideas to public awareness. She lives with her husband, fellow criminal defense lawyer John R. Muenster and their baby daughter on an island in the Puget Sound area.

Sojourns of the Soul is Kim's first book. We look forward to her second. In the meantime, we at Uni*Sun will do our best to publish books that make a real contribution to the global spiritual awakening already begun on this planet. For a free copy of our catalogue, please write to:

Uni ★ Sun
P.O. Box 25421
Kansas City, MO 64119
U.S.A